The Board Member's Easier Than You Think Guide To Nonprofit Finances

The Gold Standard in Books for Your Board

Each Can be Read in One Hour • Generous Discounts Available

Fund Raising Realities Every Board Member Must Face
David Lansdowne,
109 pp., $24.95.

After spending just one hour with this book, board members everywhere will understand virtually everything they need to know about raising major gifts. Among the top three bestselling fundraising books of all time.

The Ultimate Board Member's Book
Kay Sprinkel Grace,
110 pp., $24.95.

A book for all nonprofit boards: those wanting to operate with maximum efficiency, those needing to clarify exactly what their job is, and those wanting to ensure that all members are "on the same page." It's all here in jargon-free language.

Great Boards for Small Groups
Andy Robinson
109 pp., $24.95.

Does your board need clearly defined objectives, meetings with more focus, broader participation in fundraising, more follow-through between meetings? Say hello to your guide Andy Robinson, who offers fog-burning advice like no other board consultant.

Fundraising Mistakes that Bedevil All Boards (and Staff Too)
Kay Sprinkel Grace,
109 pp., $24.95.

Fundraising mistakes are a thing of the past. If you blunder from now on, it's simply evidence you haven't read Grace's book, in which she exposes the 44 costly errors that thwart us time and time again.

Asking
Jerold Panas, 108 pp., $24.95.

It ranks up there with public speaking. Nearly all of us fear it. Yet it's critical to the success of our organizations. Asking for money. It doesn't take steller sales skills to be an effective asker. Nearly everyone can do it if they follow Jerold Panas' step-by-step guidelines.

The Fundraising Habits of Supremely Successful Boards
Jerold Panas, 108 pp., $24.95.

Jerold Panas has observed more boards at work than perhaps anyone in America, all the while helping them to surpass their goals of $100,000 to $1 million. Here he shares what he has learned about boards that excel at resource development.

How to Make Your Board Dramatically More Effective, Starting Today
Gayle Gifford, 114 pp., $24.95.

How do you transform a good board into a great one? You have your board ask themselves the right questions. Questions like: Does our vision matter? Are we having an impact? Is our organization worthy of support? Gayle Gifford examines each key question.

How to Raise $500 to $5000 From Almost Anyone
Andy Robinson, 109 pp.,
$24.95.

It's true. You can raise $500 to $5000 from practically anyone by following Andy Robinson's advice. He's been in the trenches. He knows what works. Andy pulls no punches while at the same time according great respect to donors.

The Board Member's Easier Than You Think Guide To Nonprofit Finances

ANDY ROBINSON

NANCY WASSERMAN

First printed in October 2011

Printed in the United States of America

ISBN 978-1-889102-43-6

10 9 8 7 6 5 4 3 2 1

This text is printed on acid-free paper.

Copies of this book are available from the publisher at discount when purchased in quantity for boards of directors or staff.

Emerson & Church, Publishers
15 Brook Street • Medfield, MA 02052
Tel. 508-359-0019 • www.emersonandchurch.com

Library of Congress Cataloging-in-Publication Data

Robinson, Andy, 1957-
The board member's easier-than-you-think guide to nonprofit finances / Andy Robinson & Nancy Wasserman.
p. cm.
ISBN 978-1-889102-43-6 (pbk. : alk. paper) 1. Nonprofit organizations—Finance. 2. Nonprofit organizations—Accounting. 3. Nonprofit organizations—Management. 4. Boards of directors. I. Wasserman, Nancy, 1955- II. Title.
HG4027.65.R626 2011
658.15—dc23

2011018913

"An investment in knowledge always pays the best interest."

—Benjamin Franklin

Contents

CHAPTER 1

What Every Board Member Should Know, And Probably Doesn't

I ran into a friend in the grocery store recently. We were hanging out in the aisle, chatting about our neighbors and families, when the conversation turned to a local nonprofit.

"Aren't you on the board of Neighbors Helping Neighbors?" I asked.

"Yeah, about a year now."

"I know a little about them, but I'd like to know more. How big's your budget?"

"Last year, about $325,000. We're aiming for $350,000 this year."

"And how do you raise the money?"

"Well," she said, "about half comes from the state, a quarter from the city and county, and the rest from foundations and individual donors, including 5 percent we raise at our annual dinner. Would you like to buy a ticket?" she asked, raising an eyebrow.

"Of course," I said, laughing. "But first, tell me where the money goes."

"We're a social service agency, so the biggest line item is salaries. It's about 70 percent of the budget. The rest goes to rent, utilities, accounting, staff development, the usual stuff. We also pay mileage for volunteers, because they do a *lot* of driving. We like to say 85 percent of the money we raise goes to program costs."

Since fundraising is my business and she was asking for a gift, I pressed a little further. "Do you have a reserve fund?"

"Not formally, but we try to have money available to manage our cash flow," she said. "Our goal is to have enough cash in the bank to cover expenses for three months, in case our government funding is reduced or delayed. We're a little short of the goal, but if our event is a big success, we plan to rebuild our reserves. Now about that ticket . . . ."

► ► ►

As you might have guessed, this conversation never really happened. But as nonprofit advocates and consultants who have spent a collective fifty years working with a variety of organizations, we still dream about the perfect trustee—and when it comes to financial management skills, our fictional board member comes pretty close. We can debate all the dimensions of board leadership—strategic planning, program oversight, serving as ambassadors on behalf of the organization, and so on—but one essential aspect is written into the law governing nonprofit organizations: *fiduciary responsibility.*

These are big words, and they don't mean simply approving a budget or signing off on an audit. In the deepest sense, accepting fiduciary responsibility means integrating financial thinking, including stewardship of your assets, into every aspect of board governance. If you don't know the financial information by heart—if you're not *steeped* in the numbers and understand why they're important—it's impossible to exercise that responsibility.

So imagine we bump into each other and I start asking about your organization. Could you answer the following questions—or would you turn and run?

- What is your organization's annual budget?
- What are your current sources of income—and what would be the *best* mix of income for your organization?
- What are your largest expenses? What percentage of the budget do they consume?
- Does your organization have a reserve fund? How much is in it, and under what circumstances can it be used?
- What is your biggest financial risk?

- How do you use financial management tools to measure your impact? Does your organization compute the cost per unit of service, for example, for each client you help, or audience member you entertain, or acre you protect?
- What would help you understand your organization's financial situation more clearly?

These questions are included in a quiz for board members (see Appendix E). If you can answer them with confidence and clarity, and do so without shuffling through a pile of papers, please pass this book along to a colleague—and consider mentoring that person in the joys of financial management.

If you can't, please keep reading.

CHAPTER 2

Where Did All the Money Go?

When Things Go Horribly Wrong, Part 1

Roger was the kind of guy who's easy to like—articulate, well-organized, collaborative, and respected by his peers. He built strong relationships with a wide range of funders, was good at developing and writing grant proposals, and consequently raised a lot of money. After eight years with his environmental nonprofit, he was promoted from grant writer to executive director. He was seasoned, smart, committed to the mission. A known quantity.

Within two years of being promoted, Roger was arrested and charged with embezzling more than $150,000. His board of directors was forced to answer a host of embarrassing questions from their organization's members, funders, and especially the news media.

According to the local paper, the *Medford Mail-Tribune*, here's how Roger did it: "He opened an unauthorized account in the name of [the organization] at a local branch of Bank of America. . . . He was listed as sole signatory on the account. . . . No board member or other staff member authorized the account. Opening that unauthorized, secret account enabled him to skirt the routine steps the nonprofit group had taken to prevent financial mischief, such as requiring a second signature on transactions."

The article continues, "[He] knew which grant applications had been sent out and which checks to expect. He intercepted the checks at the mailbox before anyone else knew they had arrived, let alone been applied for, then diverted them to the hidden account. . . . He would then tell the board the grant request had been rejected."

Regrettably, Roger's story is more common than you realize. Consider Pastor Ralph, who was sentenced to six months in jail for stealing

$130,000 his congregation had donated in support of the poor. He looted the collection plate and wrote checks on the church's account. Instead of helping with food, rent, utilities, and medical bills, the money was spent on strippers, cocaine, and video poker. As one parishioner told a reporter for the *Oregonian*, "We trusted him as the ultimate role model."

His response to the congregation, as reported in the newspaper: "Will you accept my apology? Will you forgive me as Christ forgave?"

The answer was a resounding no. Last they heard, Pastor Ralph was looking for another pulpit in another state—leaving many to wonder whether he'd try the same scam all over again.

A recent Google search on the words "nonprofit embezzlement" generated 348,000 hits, including news stories from nearly every state. These results are even more remarkable when you consider that the vast majority of incidents aren't reported to police—most organizations are embarrassed and don't want to damage their reputations—and consequently never make the news.

According to a report by the Association of Certified Fraud Examiners, the world's largest anti-fraud organization, for-profit U.S companies lose 7 percent of their income to employee fraud. Perhaps nonprofits are faring better; perhaps not. To quote *Blue Avocado* (www.blueavocado.org), an online publication for nonprofits, "Imagine if we budgeted seven percent of our budgets for fraud loss!"

We don't know how much money is raised directly by nonprofit trustees, but after consulting with thousands of organizations that struggle with the perennial question, "How can we get our board to help with fundraising?" we doubt it adds up to 7 percent of total revenues. In other words, many nonprofits may be losing more to employee fraud than they're bringing in through the collective (if often ineffective) fundraising efforts of their volunteer boards. This fact puts the term *fiduciary responsibility* in a whole new light.

CHAPTER 3

Where Did All the Money Come From?

When Things Go Horribly Wrong, Part 2

Rita wasted many months betting on a grant that never came. In her responsibility as executive director, she distributed financial statements and discussed the budget at every board meeting. Each report included an update on a specific foundation, which for several years had provided more than half of the organization's annual budget.

"They invited a proposal for a renewal grant and we submitted it last month," Rita said with a confident smile.

At the next quarterly meeting, she informed her board, "They expect to make a decision soon. I talked with the program officer last week and she was encouraging."

Three months later: "Haven't heard yet," Rita told the board. "They're reorganizing and all grant decisions are on hold."

How was she keeping the ship afloat? The board didn't ask. They later discovered Rita had secretly emptied her retirement account to cover expenses. She went months without a paycheck. By the time this story ended, she was out $40,000 in retirement funds and thousands of dollars in unpaid back wages.

If Rita sounds like a saint, consider this: In collusion with the bookkeeper, she was also using a variety of tricks to hide the truth from the board. Total debt exceeded $140,000, including nearly $60,000 owed to the IRS and state tax agencies. When the board finally learned the truth, Rita lost her job and any hope of recovering her money. (By the way, board members are personally liable for unpaid payroll taxes.)

I know this story well because I served on that board. And before joining, I asked a lot of questions of Rita, other trustees, and even colleagues at similar nonprofits: Is this an effective organization? Is it well run? Why me—what can I offer that would be helpful?

But I neglected to ask very basic questions, because they seemed, well, so basic. Such as: Is the bookkeeper the only person preparing and reviewing the financial statements? Unfortunately, the answer was *yes*. Does more than one person reconcile the bank statements? The answer was *no*, unless you include the aforementioned colluding bookkeeper. Has there ever been an external audit? Another *no*. And so on.

Raising money always takes effort, but I can assure you from personal experience that the hardest money to raise is for debt relief—especially when you owe the IRS. Once we paid the tax bill and did our best to settle with other creditors, the board transferred the most viable programs to other nonprofits and dissolved the organization.

When employees steal money, we call that embezzlement. But what do we call it when an employee *pours money into the organization* or goes months without a paycheck—and nobody knows? We might start with the word *martyrdom*.

In our experience, this behavior is more common than many realize—especially in grassroots organizations. Staff members commonly skip payroll when cash flow is down, waiting to be paid after the big fundraising event or when the grant comes through. Sometimes, as Rita did, they provide personal loans to cover organizational expenses. This is problematic for a number of reasons, most of them obvious. When employees treat organizational funds like a personal piggybank—putting money in on their own initiative, then taking it out to repay themselves—it's both illegal and unethical.

At other times, often during a crisis, a particularly committed trustee will step up with a gift or loan to balance the budget. If this happens once, most would call it generosity. If it happens repeatedly, however, all that philanthropy starts to look like a rescue complex. It makes it easier for everyone to sit on the sidelines and cheer. Why should we bother to raise money, say the other trustees, when The Generous One will bail us out once again?

Let's acknowledge that in both of these scenarios, staff and board members usually have good intentions, but they're standing at the edge of a slippery slope. Some are already sliding down, ego first. These tend to be the same people who reflexively refer to the nonprofit as "my organization," and then behave as if they own it.

The punch line to Rita's story isn't what you'd expect. Yes, we flunked the part about financial controls, but as board members we failed an even bigger test of fiduciary responsibility: We didn't question the sustainability of an organization that received more than half of its budget from one funder. Any one of us could have said, "Why are we relying so much on a single grant? If we lose that grant, we're in deep trouble. What are we each willing to do—personally—to diversify our funding?"

Good board governance isn't simply about financial controls and legal responsibilities. At a deeper level, it's about building organizations that are fiscally sound *and* financially sustainable—and that includes building a diverse and generous mix of income.

CHAPTER 4

Managing Money Is Managing Mission

It's easy to say that without money, there is no mission, but that's not entirely true. Hundreds of thousands of "kitchen table" groups, without paid staff or regular expenses, enrich our communities by organizing youth programs, fighting economic or environmental threats to their neighborhoods, worshiping together, forming sports leagues, and gathering to play music. They don't worry much about fundraising or financial management since they're powered primarily by love, hope, and a lot of volunteer labor.

However, once organizations rise to the level of multiple programs, a variety of income sources, and paid staff—even if it's a lonely part-time executive director trying to juggle several tasks from a home office or a one-room storefront—everything changes. Or at least it should. Because once you're faced with payroll and other regular expenses, money—the getting, saving, tracking, allocating, and spending of it—suddenly becomes a much bigger deal.

This isn't a fundraising book, so we won't hammer away (too much) at the board's responsibility to raise money. Suffice it to say that if you're only worried about how it's spent, you're only doing half your job. As Kim Klein writes in *Reliable Fundraising in Unreliable Times*, "The instinct of many people is to cut expenses rather than raise money. . . . Resist this reflex as much as possible."

However, we need to make a more subtle and possibly more important point. How you raise your money, and how you manage it, has a lot to do with your ability to define your programs and ultimately your identity as a nonprofit.

I recently asked the director of an advocacy group, "Who owns your organization?"

"Our members," she said proudly.

"What percentage of your budget comes from membership dues and donations?"

She looked a bit uneasy. "Maybe 10 or 15 percent."

"Where does the rest come from?"

"Several foundations, plus a little from the state."

"And how does that make you feel?" I asked, noticing her discomfort.

"Vulnerable," she said, adding, "if the funders change their priorities. . . ." Her voice trailed off. "We'd like to have a little more control over our financial future."

Her members had a lot of influence over the organization's goals and programs and budget, but—given the group's dependence on grants—the external funders had at least as much, based on what they were willing to fund and what they weren't.

What may be even less well understood is this: How you manage your money can also influence your identity as well as your impact. If you don't hold your organization to the highest fiscal standards—in other words, if you join the long list of nonprofits embarrassed by financial scandals—imagine what can happen to your reputation. Because regardless of who pays for it—members, foundations, government agencies, corporations, major donors, customers, whomever—if you've been granted 501(c)(3) nonprofit status, your organization is accountable to the community at large.

That means your nonprofit's IRS return is *public information.* (If you don't believe this, visit www.guidestar.org). If anyone asks to see it—say, a donor or funder who wants to examine your financial statements—you're required to provide a copy. For this reason, your financial management systems must be as accurate, transparent, and bulletproof as possible.

As a board member, you're the final overseer of how the money is raised, invested, transferred, tracked, and spent. Your ability to manage money says a lot about your ability to manage everything else: programs, services, personnel, even your messaging. Because if you can't keep track of the money, how will you know if you're having the impact you want to have?

CHAPTER 5

Learning a New Language

Financial Management Isn't Really about Math

It won't surprise you to hear us say that financial management is a weak link in many organizations. Planning and budgeting combine all the money taboos with that common disorder, math phobia. Put a spreadsheet in front of many nonprofit leaders, and they'll run screaming from the room.

As the Institute for Conservation Leadership (ICL, www.icl.org) says in its guidebook for executive directors, "The biggest barrier to good financial management isn't mathematical ability or accounting know-how, it's attitude. For many of us, accounting and financial management are downright intimidating. The language of professional accounting—'accounts receivable, temporarily deferred income,' and the like—tend to make it so."

The language reference is instructive. Some of us have a natural gift for learning foreign languages, others have to work harder. But for anyone who has struggled to master Spanish, Chinese, or English as a second language, there comes a moment (perhaps a series of moments) when things begin to click.

Instead of laboriously translating each word in your head, the words just arrive. As you gain more practice, they come to you in phrases or complete sentences. Pretty soon you're ordering off the menu, reading the weather forecast, asking for directions, and telling stories. When you nod off to sleep and start dreaming in your second or third language, your relationship with that language grows deeper.

The ICL guidebook offers (and debunks) several myths, which are adapted below with permission.

▸ Myth 1

Attention to finances detracts from the real work.

So many nonprofit advocates and program managers, not to mention board members, have bifurcated brains: program work and advocacy on one side, money on the other. Our goal with this book is to dissolve that barrier and help you integrate your thinking.

Skilled staff members use financial data to track program results and assess their cost-effectiveness and efficacy compared to other options. As a trustee, access to this information helps you provide appropriate oversight. If you can't track and measure your impact, how will you know if your work is working, or whether you're using funds as effectively and efficiently as you'd like?

▸ Myth 2

Only people who understand finances need to look at the numbers.

Maybe you don't know anything about electricity, but you're smart enough to call an electrician when the lights go out. Throwing a party for fifty people? Find a good caterer. Planning your retirement? Hey, professionals can help with that.

In each of these situations, you don't have to solve the problem yourself, but you need to know enough to be concerned, engaged, and ask good questions. For example: Am I using too many appliances at the same time? If we feed everyone steak, how much will it cost? How much money do I need to save and invest each month?

You don't need to be a CPA or Wall Street wizard to be an effective trustee. You will, however, want enough basic wisdom to participate in the financial discussions, affirm good decisions, and raise concerns.

▸ Myth 3

I don't understand the language; therefore I can't understand the concepts.

As we suggested earlier, you understand more than you realize. If you know you don't have enough money to pay the rent or staff salaries until that foundation grant is received and deposited, then you understand the principle of *cash flow.* When a family member promises to send you $50 on your birthday, that's an *account receivable.* The $600 you owe on your credit card (and why did you buy that giant television anyway?) is an *account payable.* How about if your expenses are greater than the money you bring in each month? That's what you learn from a *statement of activities.*

We'll be using and defining financial management terms throughout the book; the most important ones appear in *italics.*

CHAPTER 6

A Three-Minute Guide to Measuring Your Organization's Financial Health

So you're trying to learn a new language—financial management—while juggling all the other things that make life challenging and rewarding: family, friends, job, chores, hobbies, bills, and (if you're lucky) a vacation. Given the limited time available for board service, what are the most important things you need to know about your organization's financial situation?

Here's the three-minute drill:

Scale

How big is your organization, financially speaking? How much money do you raise and spend each year? As a board member, your role and function in a grassroots group with an annual budget of $100,000 are quite different from serving as a trustee for a $10 million institution.

Cash or Accrual?

Are your financial statements prepared on a cash or accrual basis? *Cash-based accounting* records revenues and expenses when the money comes in or goes out. It's great for showing your exact *cash position*: how much money you have at this moment. Cash-based accounting, however, can make you appear healthier than you really are. For example, that big donation immediately puffs up the bank account—which looks and feels great—but your accounting system tells you nothing about the services you're obligated to provide with that money.

Accrual-based accounting records expenses as they occur but doesn't record revenues until the service has been delivered—so you can't book that big grant as income until you've completed (and paid for) the work it's funding. For example, you receive a $10,000 grant for a series of four programs in your local school. Under an accrual accounting system, you earn $2,500 in revenue—one quarter of the total—each time you present one of the four programs. Before delivering these programs, that money is shown as *deferred revenue*, which you'll find on the liability side of the balance sheet.

A nonprofit chorus selling season tickets offers another example. Under an accrual system, season ticket income would be listed as deferred revenue, and would be earned throughout the season as subscribers attend the concerts they've paid for in advance.

As you can see, accrual-based accounting provides a more accurate picture of your financial situation, but it's more complicated to manage.

Liquidity

Is there cash in the bank? Can you pay the immediate bills, including staff salaries?

Healthy organizations have enough money to cover typical expenses for three to six months. For example, if your organization typically spends $20,000 per month, it's prudent to have *working capital* of at least $60,000 in the bank.

Your goal, obviously, is to have enough cash to give you some flexibility. If a grant doesn't come through or you're faced with a financial surprise, ready cash buys you time to develop and implement Plan B without entering panic mode.

Let's take a look at Neighbors Helping Neighbors, the organization we introduced in Chapter 1. The nonprofit's *balance sheet* is shown on the next page. Compare their *current assets*—cash in the bank plus any assets that will become cash in the next year—to their *current liabilities*—everything that must be paid within a year, including bills, salary, and vacation time owed to their employees.

Neighbors Helping Neighbors
Balance Sheet
As of December 31, 20—

ASSETS	
Current Assets	
Checking	$70,430
Contracts and gifts receivable	17,500
Other current assets	5,000
Prepaid rent	1,500
Investments	72,000
Total current assets	166,430
Fixed assets	
Equipment	36,000
Building improvements	20,000
Total fixed assets	56,000
Total Assets	$222,430
LIABILITIES & EQUITY	
Liabilities	
Current liabilities	
Vacation and sick leave payable	$10,500
Payroll liabilities	5,600
Accounts payable	15,000
Deferred revenues	34,000
Total current liabilities	65,100
Long-term liabilities (loan balance due)	47,000
Total liabilities	112,100
Net Assets (equity)	
Restricted (per donor intent)	50,000
Unrestricted	60,330
Total net assets	110,330
Total liabilities and equity	$222,430

Their current assets (circled) are more than twice their current liabilities (also circled), which is a healthy ratio. If current assets were equal to or less than current liabilities, that would indicate a liquidity problem.

Solvency

Are you worth anything? If you shut down tomorrow, would you have anything left to pass along to another nonprofit (when nonprofits are dissolved, they're required to give their assets to another tax-exempt organization), or would you still owe your staff or vendors? Your financial *balance sheet* will help answer this question.

In the example on the previous page, the next to last line shows *total net assets*. In this case, if Neighbors Helping Neighbors had to close its doors today, the organization would be worth $110,330, at least on paper. Note that *worth* is not just cash in the bank but includes other assets such as equipment, vehicles, or property.

Profitability

Year by year, are you generating more money than you're spending? For nonprofit organizations, the notion of *profit* might seem inappropriate, but if you're consistently paying out more than you're bringing in, your group won't last long.

This point raises the question of *sustainability*: can you keep operating in the same fashion over the long term? If not—if you run a long-term deficit, losing money year after year—you obviously need to change the way you do business.

Efficiency

How well do you use your money? How do you know? In your particular field, what are the standard measurements?

Let's say you serve on the board of your local food bank, which collects food and distributes it to agencies serving the hungry. Food banks use several calculations to measure their efficiency, including the amount of food delivered for each dollar raised. For example, the national network

Feeding America provides ten pounds of food to member food banks for each dollar the organization raises, which is pretty impressive.

Youth mentoring programs track the cost of each adult-child match. Revolving loan funds calculate the expense of managing each dollar they lend to local businesses and nonprofits. Mental health agencies compute the cost per client served.

In these fields, as in many others, there are measurements or benchmarks for tracking how efficiently funds are used. While benchmarks for similar organizations can vary by geography, population served, or depth of services, it's still helpful to know and track the relevant benchmarks for your type of organization.

Impact

Are you doing what you set out to do? Are you getting the results you hope to achieve? How do you measure those results in ways that are *not* financial?

For example, FareStart is a Seattle nonprofit offering culinary training for the homeless. The organization tracks the number of alumni who find jobs. They are justifiably proud that more than 80 percent of their graduates are employed within ninety days of completing the program.

Your finances may look great, but if you're not changing lives, promoting human rights, providing compassionate care to elders, presenting great theater, improving public policies, and the like, good financial management is almost irrelevant. So if your nonprofit creates a measurable impact but your finances are a mess, imagine how much more effective you'll be once you get your financial house in order.

CHAPTER 7

It's Easier Than You Think

Creating a One-Page Financial Dashboard

You've got a board meeting tomorrow night. Because you're a diligent trustee, you've saved time to review the materials sent by the staff.

After brewing some coffee, turning off your cell phone, and finding a quiet place to work, you pick up the board packet—and your heart sinks. Half a pound of paper! Program reports, grant summaries, staff reports, news clippings, and pages and pages of financial data. You wade through the pile, pouring a second cup of coffee. Your brain goes numb.

There has to be a simpler way, right? Happily, there is.

For many nonprofits, the most critical information about finances and performance can fit on one page. This fact doesn't reduce the value of appropriate (and selectively presented) background information, but wouldn't it be great to have a one-page scorecard—a *dashboard*, as some call it—that provides a snapshot of how your organization is doing right now, plus some historical trends?

Let's return to our friends at Neighbors Helping Neighbors. This invented group recruits and coordinates volunteers to provide social services for seniors—meal delivery, transportation to doctors, yard work, home repair, companionship—across a five-county region. They also organize senior citizens to advocate for policies that help them remain in their homes and receive the government-funded services they need.

A one-page dashboard for this organization, tracking financial data, program efficiency, and impact, might look like the one on the following page. (*Note:* The numbers below were created for "Neighbors Helping Neighbors" based on the financial statements used throughout the book, and do not necessarily reflect industry standards except as indicated.)

As you can see, everything fits nicely on one page. Still, there's a lot to absorb here. Trustees who take a close look at this dashboard might raise a number of questions.

- Why are we more than $28,000 in the hole so far this year? Do we need to change our fundraising strategy or reduce expenses, or is this a predictable cash-flow problem? (For example, your group may be waiting for reimbursement from a state grant program that's typically paid toward the end of your fiscal year.)
- What can we do to increase our cash reserves?
- What's our strategy for reducing our reliance on grants and raising more unrestricted income?
- How does our cost-per-client served and cost-per-volunteer managed compare with similar organizations? What can we learn from our peers?
- Is it getting harder to recruit volunteers? Do we need to restructure the volunteer program to make it easier for people to participate?
- Our budget is gradually growing, but our client load is down this year. Why? Does this change reflect a reduction in need, an increase in costs, a reduction in revenue, a weak outreach program—or a conscious choice to serve fewer people?

Note the altitude of the questions that come from reviewing a one-page dashboard like the example above. Rather than fixating on specific line items—"Why are we spending so much on insurance?"—a dashboard prompts you to focus on the bigger picture and address issues such as financial strategy, sustainability, and effectiveness.

Indicator	How measured	What it tells you	2 years ago final	Last year final	This year target	Year to date 8 mos
FINANCIAL						
Annual budget	Total expenses	*Scale:* What our work costs	$307,200	$323,550	$ 325,500	$236,602
Net income () = loss/deficit	Total revenue minus total expenses	*Profitability:* Do revenues exceed expenses? Goal is positive number	$12,540	$4,190	$240	$(28,427)
Months cash on hand	Cash on hand/operating expenses per month	*Liquidity:* Uncommitted cash, goal is at least three months cash on hand	2.53	2.39	2.36	1.52
Net worth (or net assets or fund balance)	Total equity: assets if everything is sold	*Solvency:* Goal is positive number	$106,640	$110,330	$108,820	$91,903
Restricted income	Share of total budget for restricted uses	Flexibility in budgeting. Goal varies by group; 67% or less is good target	90%	85%	85%	88%
Govt funding as percent of total income	Govt grants and contracts total income	*Dependency:* Reliance on government funding, which can be unpredictable	85%	81%	77%	75%
EFFICIENCY						
Cost per client served	Total expenses/total clients	Efficiency in providing services	$1,299	$1,123	$1,415	$1,127
Cost per volunteer	Total volunteer costs (includes training, coordination)/number of volunteers	Efficiency of using volunteers, who are not "free" labor	$659	$625	$606	$758
IMPACT						
Number clients served	Unduplicated clients	*Reach:* Given aging population, goal is 10% increase per year	250	288	230	210
Number of volunteers engaged	Unduplicated volunteers	*Reach:* Given higher demand, goal is 15% increase per year	78	85	90	75
Average client contact hours per month	Total hours, staff plus vols/ number of clients	*Depth:* Assumes that more time equals deeper service	5.07	5.12	5.00	4.51
Number of clients still living at home	Annual tracking	*Impact:* Are we succeeding at our overall goal?	197	255	210	205

CHAPTER 8

Diversify Your Income

Managing Risk, Part 1

As you'll remember from Chapter 3, I had the unfortunate experience of serving on the board of an end-stage nonprofit. The cause of death: over-reliance on a single funder. When after multiple delays the grant wasn't renewed, the organization went down. It was a painful, messy process and could have been prevented by better board leadership in developing a comprehensive, diversified fundraising plan.

Nonprofits fail for a number of reasons, but one of the most common is a narrow funding base: relying on a limited number of grants, government contracts, or lead donors. Groups with a diverse mix of income are better positioned to handle a variety of challenges: the retirement of a founder (or a founder who won't go away), competition, a weak economy, changes in leadership, a shift in demand for services, or even the loss of a big grant or contract.

What follows is a summary of all the ways a nonprofit can generate income. (The list is adapted from the second edition of Andy's book, *Grassroots Grants.*) Not every organization can or should use every strategy, but it's still helpful to know your options.

Individuals

- Membership/donor programs
- Major gifts
- Online giving
- Monthly giving through electronic funds transfer or credit/debit cards
- Benefit events: dinners, auctions, walk-a-thons, and so on

- Workplace giving: United Way, EarthShare, Combined Federal Campaign
- Planned gifts: bequests, life insurance policies, trusts, real property, and so forth

Grants

- Foundations
- Corporations
- Public charities
- Government: federal, state, regional, county, municipal
- Service clubs: Rotary, Kiwanis, Soroptimist, and the like
- Labor unions
- Faith-based, ranging from local congregations to national funding programs

Earned Income

- Goods
- Services
- Publications
- Investment income
- Cause-related marketing and business partnerships

As a trustee, it's your responsibility to know your organization's current income mix and also the optimal mix. What combination of fundraising goals and strategies can best ensure your financial health and create the basis for sustainable growth?

This is a complex question, with implications that extend beyond fundraising. It requires an ongoing conversation among board and staff about the costs and benefits of each income strategy, how each one fits with your mission and programs, and how you allocate resources to raise money.

Consider the following scenarios, including the questions that a savvy trustee might ask:

- You raise 80 percent of your budget from a variety of grants, with no single, dominant funder. Your grantmaker relationships are strong, and you have several multi-year commitments, but few people in the community know you exist. Under these conditions, does it make sense to launch a big annual fundraising event? Do the benefits of greater visibility and donor cultivation outweigh the risk of spending more money than you bring in? Can the staff and volunteer time required to produce the event be put to better use?
- Your two primary funders have notified you that they're pulling out in two years. How can you turn this potential crisis into an opportunity? (Here's an idea: ask that a portion of the funding be designated as challenge grants to be matched by community donations. This could be a great strategy to ramp up your major gifts program.)
- Consulting and training income cover a substantial portion of your budget, but the total hasn't increased in years. How can you repackage your expertise or better promote your services to generate more money from fees?
- Twenty generous families contribute $5,000 or more annually. The executive director, however, is the only contact person for fifteen of the twenty. What will you do if he takes a job in another community?
- Three different foundations provide primary funding, but the same elderly trustee—your champion—is an officer on all three boards. Sooner or later she will pass away, and you'll lose your biggest fan. How do you reduce the risk?

In Appendix A, you'll find an income-planning form that will help you begin to create a fundraising plan that outlines your strategies, goals, deadlines, and assignments. All trustees need to understand the broad outlines of this plan and their individual roles in implementing it—customized to suit their skills, temperament, and available time.

If the board neither understands nor embraces the plan, your fundraising will sputter. An uninformed board member might tell the staff, "Go write another grant proposal." Compare this statement with the responsible trustee who asks, "What are our options? What are the benefits and risks of each option? What can I do to help?"

CHAPTER 9

Financial Controls

Managing Risk, Part 2

If you've spent time in airports, you've undoubtedly seen unaccompanied minors. Maybe they're off to see Grandma, or heading to summer camp, or shuttling between parents who live in different cities.

Airlines have elaborate procedures for handing these children from one responsible adult to the next: from parent to check-in staff to gate agent to flight attendant to gate agent to Grandma. When they're not on planes, the kids are herded from one secure holding area to another. Every movement and handoff is tracked. If the system fails, as it rarely does, it's big news.

When we talk about financial controls, it might be useful to think about all the ways your organization can receive, hold, or spend money (grant payments, bank accounts, credit cards, and so forth) as unaccompanied children. Without appropriate procedures, and without designated people engaged throughout the process, money can be misdirected or embezzled.

Effective financial controls have three attributes: they ensure safe care of your assets; divide responsibilities among several people; and are fully disclosed to, and understood by, all concerned parties.

Let's begin with *custody of assets*: The first step is to create strong *physical controls* in the workplace. All your cash and the means of transferring it—checks, bank account numbers, passwords, petty cash, credit card numbers, and even the cards themselves—should be locked up.

Sounds obvious, right? Well, we recently learned about an enterprising nonprofit employee who took a few blank checks each month from the box of extra checks, forging the executive director's signature before cashing them. A total of $11,000 disappeared. Now the only people with keys to the check drawer are the executive director and the treasurer.

And we're not just talking about physical assets, such as credit cards. Secure your computers—especially those containing financial software—with passwords and restricted access. Use lockouts to close computer programs when staff members are away from their desks. Back up important data regularly and store it off-site.

The second principle of good financial controls is *separation of duties* so that multiple people are involved in most transactions, making it harder for someone to run off with the money. Smaller organizations commonly ignore this principle, which can lead to disaster.

A sad-but-true story: A parent-teacher organization in the Pacific Northwest was raising money for a middle school field trip through the usual means—bake sales, car washes, and raffles. One volunteer parent handled all financial duties, including depositing cash and reconciling the bank statements. When she needed money for personal expenses, she secretly borrowed from the account, then paid it back. After a while, she stopped paying it back. By the time the crime was discovered, this well-meaning volunteer had stolen $10,000, and the field trip was cancelled.

How did this happen? No one else ever looked at the bank statements.

To create appropriate separation of duties, many organizations require board approval for expenditures above a certain amount, and may also require two signatures on checks. (Beware: banks sometimes disregard your two-signature policy and will cash the check anyway.)

If the bookkeeper prepares checks to pay the bills and records payments, someone else should sign the checks. Ideally, a third person receives the *unopened* bank statement (or has a unique password for online access) to reconcile the account. In small to mid-sized organizations, that third person is often the volunteer treasurer.

Remember the theft we described earlier, with the employee who stole checks from the box of extras? The treasurer, a financial professional, was well qualified and reasonably diligent but was literally unavailable for three months during tax season. During that time, nobody reconciled the accounts. Guess which months the enterprising staff member—who had a degree in criminal justice!—chose to steal and forge those unlocked checks?

In cases where the executive director or finance director prepares financial statements, the finance committee or treasurer should review the numbers before presentation to the full board. These outside eyes often find discrepancies: "How come our travel expenses tripled last month?" or "We have $4,000 in miscellaneous expenses; what does that mean?"

Separation of duties should be incorporated into your entire chain of financial actions, from authorizing, executing, and recording expenditures through receiving, recording, and depositing income. Ask yourselves: In our organization, where are the weak links in the chain? Where are our assets most likely to be lost or stolen, and how do we separate duties to protect ourselves better?

The third principle of good financial controls is *transparency*. In exchange for serving the public good, nonprofits are exempt from most state and federal taxes. Because your group literally belongs to the community, your IRS returns and other government filings are public information.

Like it or not, everybody knows your business. Smart organizations embrace this reality and use it to their advantage. For example, many organizations receiving high marks on rating services such as Charity Navigator—these services evaluate your nonprofit, in large part, by reviewing your government paperwork—tout their scores to show that they use money efficiently.

Begin by clarifying who does what, so everyone on the staff and board understands your financial system. Create a flow chart or map showing how money moves through your organization, both in and out, and who is responsible at each stage. On the following page you'll find an example for handling income that might work well for a small organization with a limited number of staff.

This is bit like the airline employee informing the parent, "I'm going to bring Johnny through security myself. When we get to the gate Maria takes over; she's the gate agent. She'll keep an eye on him until he's safely on the plane. From there, the lead flight attendant will take care of him until they land in Los Angeles."

An outside accountant can help you build a culture of transparency within your organization. Accountants often raise concerns about your financial management systems, share those concerns with leadership, and assist you in making corrections and improvements. By conducting an audit certified by an accountant, you announce to the world that you strive to manage your finances effectively, you welcome professional scrutiny, and you have nothing to hide.

If your organization is affiliated with a larger network, you may be required or encouraged to meet standards set by the national office. The Planned Parenthood Federation of America has a rigorous review process for local affiliates that covers a variety of business practices, including financial management and board governance. The Land Trust Alliance offers voluntary certification for local and regional land trusts. Peer reviews such as these add another level of credibility to your work; your staff should know if something similar exists for your category of nonprofit.

Like Johnny's reunion with Grandma, the nuts and bolts of financial controls are largely invisible unless they fail. As a board member, your job is not to manage the system but to oversee the policies that ensure all the necessary pieces are in place.

For an overview of nonprofit financial roles—who does what?—plus a checklist to keep track of assignments, take a look at Appendices B and C.

Separation of Duties

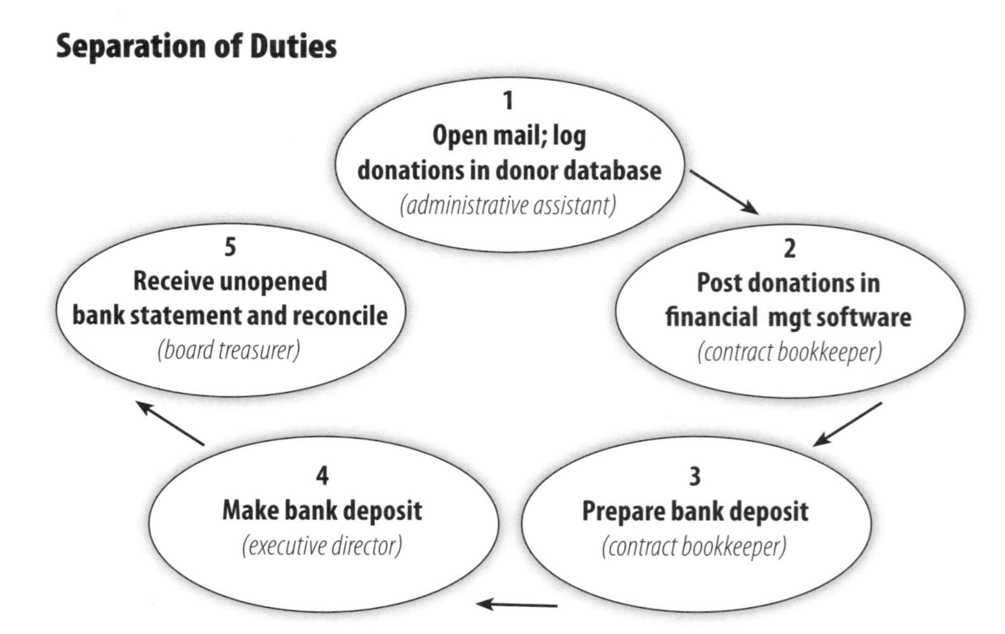

CHAPTER 10

Insurance and Other Necessities

Managing Risk, Part 3

The spare tire in your trunk is more or less invisible until you need it—and when you need it, on that dark and stormy night, you better have it. The same principle holds true for the flashlight in the kitchen drawer (when the power goes out) or that fire extinguisher hanging in the pantry.

Like a spare tire or a fire extinguisher, insurance is one of those things you must have but hope you never need. According to Pamela Davis, president and CEO of the Nonprofit Insurance Alliance Group (www.insurancefornonprofits.org), most organizations require at least three kinds of coverage:

- *General liability*, which covers injuries and property damage suffered by visitors, clients, and customers.
- *Non-owned/hired auto insurance*, which provides additional coverage for employees who use their own vehicles on the job.
- *Directors and officers*, known as *D&O*, which protects the organization's board members—for example, if an unhappy former employee sues for wrongful termination or a big donor claims you mismanaged his gift. The NIAG reports that about 4 percent of nonprofits will have a D&O claim in any given year.

All you need is one lawsuit alleging harassment or wrongful termination to understand the value of this type of insurance.

True story: A nonprofit board sets performance benchmarks for their long-time executive director, who refuses to honor them and quits. She takes the organization to court, claiming breach of contract by arguing that the board changed the rules of employment in the middle of the game. The organization negotiates a cash settlement with the employee, the costs are covered by D&O insurance, and the board members are protected from personal liability.

In addition to these three types of insurance, state law may require you to have worker's compensation coverage for employees injured at work. And there's more if you want it.

Most organizations that own buildings, vehicles, or other equipment purchase insurance against loss and damages. Other nonprofits buy renter insurance to cover building contents, fidelity insurance for employee theft, professional liability coverage if they provide counseling or referrals, or sexual conduct insurance. You can even buy cyber insurance to cover data loss or weather insurance in case your big fundraising event is wiped out by a blizzard. Not surprisingly, you can combine several coverages under an *umbrella* policy.

In the online publication *Blue Avocado*, Pamela Davis writes, "Almost all of the claims—90 percent—reported by nonprofit organizations are accidents and injuries related to automobiles or slips, trips, and falls at nonprofit locations and special events. . . . The other 10 percent result from improper employment practices (such as wrongful termination), professional errors and omissions, and sexual abuse. While less frequent, these tend to be more difficult and expensive claims to resolve and account for 35 percent of claims dollars paid."

If you find this topic unsettling—you're envisioning paperwork, lawyers, and a bank account bleeding money—relax. Appropriate insurance coverage will spare you at least some of the stress and much of the cost, assuming you buy it first.

If you already have insurance, ask your broker to review your policies. If you don't, consider convening a board-staff team to meet with insurance professionals who serve the nonprofit community.

Once you've purchased insurance, created a diversified funding plan, and implemented a financial controls policy (Chapters 8-10), a few more items may require your attention. Every one of these topics has financial implications. If you don't have proactive plans for business continuity, site security, and data security, it can cost your organization a lot of money.

Business continuity

Imagine the worst: Your office is flooded, or there's a fire, or you're hit by a hurricane, ice storm, or earthquake. No one can get to the office for a week. Do you have off-site backups of all critical information? Do you have a telephone tree or listserv to update your employees? How will you stay in touch with your clients and customers? If your work is site-specific—you run a clinic, a theater, or an animal shelter—where will they go until you're ready to serve them again?

Site security

The first food cooperative I joined, circa 1977, was housed in a former gas station, and it was self-serve all the way. Every member had a key. You let yourself in, helped yourself to carrots and oats and chocolate chips, weighed your purchases, computed the cost, logged the total on the sales sheet, and put your money in the cash box. If you weren't too distracted by the chocolate chips, you also locked the door on the way out.

Although I appreciate the egalitarian impulse behind this business model, I can only speculate how much income was lost to random nibbling and bad arithmetic, not to mention outright theft.

Beyond locks and (a limited number of) keys, site security requirements vary widely depending on mission, geography, and the nature of your work. Domestic violence shelters operate in private locations, with stringent entry rules to protect the residents. On the other hand, if you're running a thrift store, you actually want strangers wandering in, so your security plan might focus on shoplifting (and maybe employee theft). Once you assess the risks, you can customize your approach to deal with the most likely threats.

Data security

All nonprofits operate in a digital world, and every executive director has nightmares about crashing computers and missing data. Everything you do—heal patients, sell tickets, protect animals, organize worship services, measure pollution, educate children, track legislation, raise money—has a digital component, and your work gets a lot harder when data is mangled or lost, or confidentiality is breached.

As in the other areas we've covered, it falls to the staff to sort out the logistics: passwords, networks, protection from hackers, back-up protocols, and off-site storage. The board needs to know there's a data protection plan in place, and needs enough basic expertise to monitor and evaluate the plan. In addition to the usual trustee wish list—lawyer, banker, and wealthy philanthropist—you might include a computer geek. If you're looking for an opportunity to add younger people to your board, look no further.

CHAPTER 11

Finding the Best Altitude For Financial Oversight

How Much Control Is the Right Amount?

Inexperienced boards tend to work at the wrong altitude by focusing on details better left to staff. The board's primary job is planning and oversight. The staff (assuming you have staff) implements the plan through daily operations. Board members function best as leaders: providing vision, evaluating results, overseeing the finances. In these moments they serve as guides and supervisors to the lead staff, and they're fulfilling their most important responsibility.

At other times—especially in smaller organizations—they do the work of traditional volunteers: painting the office, mentoring children, writing thank you notes, leading hikes, and dragging chairs around at the annual fundraising event. At these moments, they need to accept guidance from staff or whoever is organizing the activity and not abuse their power as trustees by undercutting or second-guessing their colleagues.

When it comes to financial management, the division of responsibilities gets a bit murkier. It's a short step from due diligence to micromanagement, and the line may shift based on staffing, budget size, or the overall health of the organization. For example, if the organization faces a fiscal crisis or has unexpectedly lost its CEO, trustees may need to step in temporarily to fill roles normally reserved for staff.

To prevent confusion about roles, it's important to clarify the chain of command. In the traditional model, the board supervises the executive director or CEO, who in turn supervises other staff, including financial staff. Noted on the next page are the most common ways boards descend into the weeds rather than maintaining the appropriate altitude.

ACTIVITY	STAFF ROLE	BOARD ROLE	WATCH OUT FOR . . .
Budgeting	Budget research	Set annual targets income and expenses	Board members who focus on specific line items and relatively small amounts
	Prepare draft budget	Amend and approve	Board members who reflexively want to cut expenses before looking for ways to diversify and increase income
Financial systems	Manage financial records, expenditures, and budgets; use systems to analyze data and report trends to the board	Use actual financial data for planning, oversight, and evaluation, rather than relying on hearsay or gut feelings about cost or performance	"We've got the wrong software, we need to use ____," rather than, "To provide appropriate oversight, we need different information than we're getting"
Expenditures	Prepare checks and other payments	Approve budget and high-cost purchases Co-sign checks (usually for larger amounts)	Board members who want to behave like the bookkeeper and handle payments
Salaries	Set salary structure and hire staff (other than ED)	Hire executive director	"Why are we paying $____ for development staff? Can't we get someone for less?"
	Authorize raises	Approve salary and benefits structure as a component of the overall budget	
Fundraising and income diversification	Develop a diversified fundraising plan reflecting budget goals and organizational needs	Understand, amend and approve the funding plan; participate in fundraising activities as assigned and expected of the board	Board members with a favorite idea they want someone else (staff) to implement, even though it's not included in the plan
Financial trouble-shooting	Identify and address day-to-day financial problems	Identify anomalies that appear in the financial reports and ask questions Provide guidance and suggestions	Board members who say "This is how we (the board) will fix the problem" rather than offering support and tools for the ED

CHAPTER 12

"Do We Really Need A Finance Committee?"

If the board views the world from high above the landscape (hence the word *oversight*) and the staff is down on the ground chopping through the underbrush, someone needs to serve as a communications link to bridge these two perspectives. The executive director and finance director help to fill this function, but when it comes to money matters, having more translators and communicators can be a good thing.

Think of the finance committee as operating at the middle altitude: high enough to see the big picture, but low enough to notice the details. In smaller organizations this role may be filled by the executive committee or even the treasurer, but as budgets grow larger and more complex, a finance committee can add a useful, arm's-length perspective.

The committee is typically responsible for the following:

1) Reviewing draft financial reports, digging beneath the numbers, asking strategic questions, and clarifying whatever is unclear. For example:

- Staff costs as a percentage of the budget just jumped from 65 percent to 75 percent over the last six months. Why?
- What happened to the bequest we received in April? I don't see it in any of these line items.
- How are the expenses of the new building reflected in the financials?
- Grants make up an increasing portion of our budget. Aren't we trying to move in the other direction?

2) As needed, translating the numbers to the board. The finance committee can train trustees to understand and use financial reports. For example, at least once per year, it would be great to devote an hour at a board meeting going through the financial statement line by line, discussing the implications of each item.

3) Serving as mentors and backstops for the executive director, especially if he or she has limited financial management expertise. In one mid-sized nonprofit, the fiscal manager left and the executive director, not knowing any better, hired a temporary employee with much weaker skills. The finance committee took one look at the latest financial reports, which were poorly prepared, and intervened. Within three months, the organization had hired a professional finance director. If the finance committee hadn't stepped up, the agency could have been caught off guard by a cash-flow crisis.

4) Reviewing the audit and interpreting it for the full board while monitoring any changes suggested by the auditor. In an eerily similar story—finance director goes on medical leave, junior employee makes a mess of the books—the deputy director, finance committee, and auditor worked together to straighten out the accounts and create policies to prevent future problems.

5) Focusing on building organizational assets and long-term financial strength, in contrast to the executive director's focus on cash flow, fundraising, and day-to-day financial needs. The finance committee can accomplish this by suggesting and monitoring policies to diversify income, increase reserves, and create an endowment, if appropriate (see Chapter 21).

6) Developing an investment strategy for your reserve fund and other cash. If you plan to use an outside investment manager, start with your local community foundation or a professional who specializes in investing for nonprofits. "There are so many horror stories about a trustee asking his brother-in-law the stock broker to manage the organization's investments,"

says nonprofit financial management consultant Kay Sohl. "These stories almost always turn out badly."

Sohl suggests asking yourselves the following questions: "Do we have anyone on the committee who knows enough to evaluate the performance of our investments? Is that person willing and able to commit the time needed to monitor our strategy? Often, the answer is no."

CHAPTER 13

Financial Conflicts of Interest

It's Not Your Money

The vast majority of board members get involved with a nonprofit organization because they're concerned about a community issue, perhaps one affecting them personally. Maybe they want to protect the local water supply, or improve their kids' education, or cure a disease affecting someone they love, or listen to a live orchestra without driving hours to the nearest big city.

In other words, self-interest isn't inherently a bad thing. It can be a powerful force for good. Still, there will be times when personal needs and desires are at odds with organizational goals, and this conflict can lead to serious problems. Add money to the equation, and things get even stickier. For example, imagine a board member who:

- Offers to sell services to the organization—accounting, investment, construction, computer, catering—and earn a profit.
- Bids on a consulting contract for the organization.
- Is willing to loan money to the organization at above-market interest rates.

These are fairly straightforward examples of conflicts of interest, because these trustees are using their board positions to profit personally—or, to reference the official IRS language, "receive an inappropriate benefit." We say "fairly straightforward," because even in these situations, the lines are a little blurred. What if the trustee offers services for free? Or at cost? Does the consultant need to resign from the board before submitting a bid? Can she simply take a leave of absence while doing the work and then return to the board?

Consider the following real-life example: A social service agency runs out of money while waiting to be reimbursed via its government grant. One of the board members offers a loan to tide them over until the government makes payment. Sounds great, right? However, the trustee's son works at the nonprofit and without the loan he might miss some paychecks. (Which makes us wonder if he'll be moving in with his parents, and how they feel about that.)

Presumably, this nonprofit could have paid more for a bank loan without raising the appearance of a conflict of interest. Cost and expedience—which are important factors—trumped other considerations. This scenario doesn't offer an obvious right or wrong answer, which is how conflicts of interest generally play out in the real world.

Sooner or later, your board will face these kinds of challenges; here's how you might prepare yourselves.

Try to define inappropriate behavior before it begins. If you're the trustee of a preschool and also a parent of a student at the school, how far can you go in advocating for a scholarship policy that might save money for your family? If you're working to conserve open space, how would you prioritize protection of adjacent land that could increase the financial value of your own property? (A few years back, The Nature Conservancy faced a lot of scrutiny on a similar question.) Talk through the implications of the choices you might have to make.

Request conflict of interest policies from sister organizations. How do other nonprofits deal with this question? What can you learn from them? For example, the Vermont Community Loan Fund requires trustees with a potential conflict of interest to leave the room when relevant topics are discussed at a board meeting.

Study relevant guidelines from professional associations and networks. If your group belongs to a peer network or is evaluated by a credentialing agency, ask for a template or a list of criteria that cover this issue. The Land

Trust Alliance, for example, offers materials and training to help land conservation organizations avoid and address conflicts of interest.

Disclose, disclose, disclose. Because your organizational reputation is your most important asset, the perception of a conflict of interest can be as damaging as a real one. The following scenarios could raise eyebrows in your community:

- The realty firm you own is listing the building your nonprofit hopes to buy.
- Your daughter is playing the lead role in your theater's summer production.
- Your best friend put in a bid for constructing the new addition to your clinic.

By disclosing these facts, you show you have nothing to hide. Transparency makes it easier for your board colleagues to suggest when it might be best for you to step away from the discussion or decision.

Name it. If you believe a trustee has crossed the line by promoting his or her financial interests, take responsibility and raise the issue. As a first step, talk with the person individually, perhaps accompanied by the board chair. If this strategy fails, bring your concerns to the full board. This step is much easier to take if trustees have discussed the topic in advance and developed guidelines.

Recuse yourself. If you and your colleagues agree that you have a conflict of interest or could be perceived as having a conflict of interest that might harm the organization, step aside while others make the relevant decision. If necessary, the board can create a benchmark to trigger this recusal. For example, if a majority of the trustees perceive a conflict of interest, the relevant board member(s) would be required to step aside for that vote or other decision-making process.

Unfortunately, if you need a vote to sort these things out, you haven't done your homework. Most problems relating to personal agendas and conflicts of interest can be resolved much sooner—through clear expectations, open conversations, and a written policy prepared before potential conflicts arise.

CHAPTER 14

Understanding and Using Financial Statements

Where Do We Stand, Where Have We Been?

In a perfect world, most of the financial information you need to fulfill your board responsibilities would fit on one page. (The model for this perfect world can be found in Chapter 7.) There are times, however, when trustees need a deeper look at the numbers, and that's when it's essential to have complete, accurate, and timely financial statements.

On the following pages, let's take a look at the two most relevant items: the balance sheet and profit and loss statement.

Neighbors Helping Neighbors
Balance Sheet
As of December 31, 20—

ASSETS	
Current Assets	
Checking	$70,430
Contracts and gifts receivable	17,500
Other current assets	5,000
Prepaid rent	1,500
Investments	72,000
Total current assets	166,430
Fixed assets	
Equipment	36,000
Building improvements	20,000
Total fixed assets	56,000
Total Assets	$222,430
LIABILITIES & EQUITY	
Liabilities	
Current liabilities	
Vacation and sick leave payable	$10,500
Payroll liabilities	5,600
Accounts payable	15,000
Deferred revenues	34,000
Total current liabilities	65,100
Long-term liabilities (loan balance due)	47,000
Total liabilities	112,100
Net Assets (equity)	
Restricted (per donor intent)	50,000
Unrestricted	60,330
Total net assets	110,330
Total liabilities and equity	$222,430

A balance sheet or statement of financial position is a snapshot of your financial situation. It shows *what you own*, *what you owe*, and *what you are worth* at that specific moment. As you can see from this example, Neighbors Helping Neighbors has total net assets of $110,330—in other words, that's what the organization is worth.

On the balance sheet, your *assets* include cash, receivables (money owed to your organization), inventory, other financial assets such as stock or bond investments, plus hard assets such as property and equipment. Your *liabilities*—in this example, $112,100—are anything you owe, including money owed to vendors, loans, and accrued payroll benefits such as vacation time and sick leave.

If you use an accrual-based accounting system, which we described in Chapter 6, your balance sheet will also show *deferred revenue*: services for which you have been paid but have not yet delivered. Neighbors Helping Neighbors has $34,000 in deferred revenue. Under this system, you can't count the money—for example, a grant—until you've completed the work that grant is funding.

In financial language, the next-to-last line on your balance sheet is referenced by many names—*fund equity, net worth, fund balance, retained earnings, total equity, total net assets*, and others—but they all mean essentially the same thing. If you sold everything (and received the full value expressed on your balance sheet), paid all your debts, and closed your doors today, how much would be left? Or would you owe money? In this example, Neighbors Helping Neighbors would be left with $110,330.

Now, on the next page let's turn to a *profit and loss (P&L)* or *statement of activities*. It's more like a movie, showing *what you earned and what you spent* over a specific period.

Neighbors Helping Neighbors

Statement of Activities

January 1 – December 31, 20—

REVENUES	
Government grants and contracts	$264,750
Foundation grants	14,800
Membership	11,027
Major gifts	17,393
Board gifts	2,500
Benefit events	14,030
Investment income (net)	3,240
Total Revenue	$327,740
OPERATING EXPENSES	
Salary and benefits	$256,386
Insurance	5,000
Miscellaneous	889
Office supplies	1,053
Postage and shipping	1,935
Printing	2,881
Professional development	3,750
Professional services	19,323
Rent and utilities	15,050
Staff/volunteer mileage and travel	15,750
Telephone and Internet	1,533
Total Operating Expenses	$323,550
Increase (decrease) in net assets (aka Net Income)	$4,190

The P&L goes by several names, including *income statement, operating statement*, and *revenue and expense statement*. In a recent annual report, the Flynn Center for Performing Arts titled their statement of activities, "Where It Came From and Where It Went"—a great example of financial plain-speak.

Typically, the financial reports created by nonprofit staff show all major revenues and expenditures, then compare actual totals to the budgeted amounts you expected to earn and spend. (See Chapters 16 and 17, which cover managing the budget.) These operating statements show how well you're sticking to the financial plan, illuminate any bumps in the road, and can provide early warning signs if you're veering away from your intended financial path.

The bottom line on a P&L shows your *net income* or *net assets*: did you make money or lose money during that time? As you can see, Neighbors Helping Neighbors had net income of $4,190.

Some boards also request *accounts payable (A/P)* and *accounts receivable (A/R)* statements, such as shown on the next page.

Accounts payable show the amounts due (and possibly overdue) to your vendors. Accounts receivable show the amount due (or possibly overdue) for services you've already provided. As you can see, Neighbors Helping Neighbors has accounts payable of $15,000 and accounts receivable of $17,500. Note that these line items also appear on the balance sheet on page 58; accounts receivable is listed as "Contracts and Gifts Receivable." A/P and A/R statements offer a more in-depth way to understand your organization's cash-flow challenges and opportunities.

Steve Gold, who was commissioner of several agencies for the state of Vermont and has served on many nonprofit boards, offers useful advice for understanding financial statements. Steve, who admits to flunking a math class in college, encourages board members to "get smart with numbers over time. The goal is to understand the implications without doing all the calculations." He urges trustees to "look for anomalies" when reviewing financial statements—the numbers that jump out because they're larger, smaller, different, or just don't make sense at first glance.

Neighbors Helping Neighbors
Accounts Payable Aging Summary
As of August 31, 20—

	Current	1–30	31–60	>60	TOTAL
OfficeSupplies.com	$250	0	0	0	$250
P & A Fuel Co.	1,725	750	0	0	2,475
Dewey & Howe, PC	5,000	2,500	2,500	0	10,000
Ready-Quik Printing	500	0	0	0	500
Anna Martin-travel reimbursement	350	150	0	0	500
Mike Shea-travel reimbursement	325	100	0	0	425
Andy Wu-travel reimbursement	200	100	25	0	325
Martina Sommers travel reimbursement	175	250	0	0	425
Sarah Pena-travel reimbursement	100	0	0	0	100
Total Revenue	$8,625	$3,850	$2,525	0	$15,000

Neighbors Helping Neighbors
Accounts Receivable Aging Summary
As of August 31, 20—

	Current	1–30	31–60	61–60	>90	TOTAL
State contract	$3,200	$4,000	$2,000	$1,500	0	$10,700
City grant	0	1,800	0	0	0	1,800
ABC Foundation	0	4,000	0	0	0	4,000
Gifts pledged	1,000	0	0	0	0	1,000
	$4,200	$9,800	$2,000	$1,500	0	$17,500

If you find irregularities or don't understand what you're looking at, ask questions. For example:

- We've got $25,000 in donor pledges receivable—90 days or more. Why are we having such a hard time collecting the money?
- Why was our payroll line 50 percent larger in March than any other month? (Possible explanation: you may have completed three payroll periods in March, rather than the typical two.)
- We just had a new database installed, but I don't see that in the computer expense line. Is the cost reflected in these statements?
- According to the balance sheet, our land is worth a lot of money, so our unrestricted net assets look really good, but we don't have much cash. How does this affect our daily operations?

These sorts of anomalies are often identified by the bookkeeper or finance director and brought to the board's attention. A colleague of ours, a former finance director, described her job as "laying a trail of bread crumbs for the board to follow." However, the prudent trustee has enough financial savvy to raise these sorts of questions without being led through them first.

CHAPTER 15

Budgets as Maps

Planning Your Future

In Chapter 5, we discussed how mastering financial management is a bit like learning a new language. You don't have to read Dostoyevsky in Russian to be an effective board member, but you do need to be fluent enough, in financial terms, to order off the menu, understand the weather forecast, ask for directions, and organize your trip.

It's a more satisfying trip if you're joined by competent staff, but staff members tend to operate at ground level. They can get lost in the daily rhythm of delivering programs, managing staff, raising money, and keeping the organization running. Given these circumstances, it falls to the trustees to keep their collective eyes on the destination. Where is your organization going and how will you get there?

When you use budgets effectively, they are maps that begin to define the territory and help you plan your way through it. An effective budget includes benchmarks allowing you to track your progress. It can also help you identify alternate routes when needed. (For a discussion of the value of contingency budgets, see Appendix D.)

As you review the budget—posing questions and making adjustments along the way—consider the following advisories:

Begin with what you want, not what you think you can get. The central tension in budget planning is the push-pull between expenses—the cost of delivering the mission—and revenues—how much money you think you can raise. Some organizations work backwards by starting with a revenue target, then try to configure their programs to fit the available income.

Unfortunately, this approach is self-fulfilling: It begins with the assumption of scarcity and then confirms that scarcity. I once served on the board of an organization whose building was literally crumbling. My colleagues were convinced we couldn't raise enough to rebuild it, so we chose to ignore gravity. When an engineer told us the building was unsafe and prohibited us from using it, we started a capital fundraising campaign because we had no choice.

The engineer's report turned out to be the proverbial blessing in disguise. Once we started asking for gifts, the community responded in unexpected, generous ways, and we now have a beautiful new facility.

So it's much healthier to start the budgeting conversation by asking, "What resources do we need to do our work really well?" rather than, "What do we have to work with?" Then ask, "How can we get those resources?" This approach better positions you to generate the money you need. Nine times out of ten, the approved budget lands somewhere between your dreams—the best-case scenario—and your fears—the worst case.

In successful organizations, the budget process also includes a funding diversification plan that is implemented, in part, through board engagement. Indeed, some nonprofits create specific line item targets for board giving (personal gifts) and board fundraising, then use the budget to track their performance. Here's the relevant line item from a New York nonprofit, Families First in Essex County:

	JAN-SEPT	ANNUAL BUDGET
Board member pledges	$2,580.00	$8,000.00

Colorado Conservation Voters goes even further, coding all membership donations (under $500) and major gifts ($500 and up) as follows: Board Give, Board Get, and Other. Using these codes makes it easy to create financial reports that track board fundraising results.

Look behind the numbers. Creating and approving budgets is about more than balancing expenses and revenues. Budgets are actually policy documents: the means for implementing your philosophy and strategy of service delivery, sustainability, staff development and compensation, and use of volunteers.

When reviewing a grant proposal, many funders flip to the budget pages first, as they provide convenient shorthand for understanding an organization's story. A skilled trustee will learn, with time and experience, to read budgets the same way. We'll discuss how in more detail in the next two chapters.

How much uncertainty can you handle? This is a critical question, because budgets are aspirational documents, not guarantees. A map is only a two-dimensional representation, and once you're moving across the landscape, things always look different from what you imagined when planning the trip.

Your staff members who create the annual budget are trying to predict the future, so they estimate the numbers based on history and data and instinct and trends in the marketplace. In other words, a budget is a series of educated guesses. When you invent these numbers and put them on paper, you begin to shape an uncertain future, because these figures define your goals for both fundraising and spending.

CHAPTER 16

Managing the Budget, Part 1

Are We Heading in the Right Direction?

As we discussed in the previous chapter, even the best-planned journeys include unexpected detours. The road washes out, the tour bus gets lost, the cell phone battery dies—but look, what a lovely little restaurant on the hill, maybe we should stop for a meal? Some detours lead to trouble, while others yield unexpected opportunities.

The most important navigational skill is comparing where you are to where you expected to be, then making corrections. Consider the following budget for our friends at Neighbors Helping Neighbors, the fictional organization we've featured throughout the book. Let's begin with their income (see next page):

Each major income source is listed (this is the relevant mix for Neighbors Helping Neighbors; your income categories may be different) and tracked several ways using multiple columns.

Annual budget. When preparing the budget, the amount expected from each source.

Actual YTD (year to date) and percentage of budgeted amount. These lines provide a way of comparing budget projections to reality. Since eight months equals two-thirds of the year, ideally Neighbors Helping Neighbors would have secured at least 67 percent of their budget by now. Notice that each line item varies from the 67 percent projection, but total income to date is 64 percent of the annual goal, so they're just a little short of the target.

Income	Annual Budget	Actual YTD Jan–Aug	% of Budgeted Amount Target: 67%	Projected to year end	% of Budgeted Amount Target: 100%	Notes
State grants and contracts	$171,000	$85,000	50%	$155,000	91%	$70,000 grant payment due 9/30
City/county grants	95,000	80,500	85%	80,500	85%	Unlikely to receive more grants this year
Foundations	27,500	26,500	96%	34,500	125%	Three proposals pending
Membership	12,500	5,470	44%	15,250	122%	Assumes year-end equals last year
Major gifts	15,000	3,500	23%	20,000	133%	Major = $500+; need year-end push
Board gifts	3,500	1,550	44%	5,000	143%	Asking for more to offset state cuts
Benefit events	18,000	15,017	83%	15,017	83%	Spring benefit, final tally
Investment	3,240	2,138	66%	3,500	108%	
TOTAL	**$345,740**	**$219,675**	**64%**	**$328,767**	**95%**	

Projected to year end and Percentage of budgeted amount. These projections assume specific actions and outcomes during the last four months of the year, as referenced in the Notes column: The balance of the state grant is paid, other grant applications are funded, and the organization strengthens outreach to individual donors. The board is also asked to give a little more to help fill the gap created by reduced government funding.

Now, on the next page, let's take a look at the expense side of the budget, then the summary line. The last line, titled Net Income, should raise concerns. It shows a year-to-date deficit of $28,427 and a projected year-end deficit of $30,828.

In the next chapter, we'll go through this budget in more detail to identify questions you might ask if you were on the board. If you're comfortable with budget analysis, feel free to skip ahead to Chapter 18. If not, we encourage you to pay close attention to what follows.

Expenses	Annual Budget	Actual YTD Jan–Aug	% of Budgeted Amount Target: 67%	Projected to year end	% of Budgeted Amount Target: 100%	Notes
Salary/benefits	$247,100	$164,000	66%	$258,325	105%	Health insurance increase; unfilled position in 4th quarter
Occupancy (rent/utilities)	15,600	10,450	67%	15,600	100%	
Telephone/Internet	1,600	1,040	65%	1,550	97%	
Postage/shipping	2,000	1,355	68%	2,370	119%	Larger year-end mailing
Printing	3,000	2,834	94%	3,800	127%	Larger year-end mailing
Office supplies	1,200	451	38%	750	63%	
Staff/volunteer mileage & travel	18,800	15,750	84%	20,500	109%	Weak economy, more volunteers claiming mileage
Insurance	5,200	5,200	100%	5,200	100%	
Professional development	5,000	1,625	33%	3,200	64%	
Professional services	25,000	33,357	133%	36,000	144%	Includes legal fees; insurance will reimburse approx. $10K next year
Miscellaneous	1,000	540	54%	800	80%	
TOTAL	**$325,500**	**$236,602**	**73%**	**$348,095**	**107%**	
Reserve fund	$20,000	$11,500	58%	11,500	58%	Due to shortfall, putting less into reserves
Total plus reserve	**$345,500**	**$248,102**	**72%**	**$359,595**	**104%**	
NET INCOME	**$240**	**($28,427)**		**($30,828)**		

CHAPTER 17

Managing the Budget, Part 2

A Fork in the Road

If you carefully review the budget featured in the previous chapter, you're likely to identify at least three issues of concern. These are presented below. Following each one, we've highlighted the relevant line items to help you understand why and how these are key questions a trustee might ask when presented with this budget.

1. *Why are we more than $28,000 in the hole so far this year?* This is a bigger deficit than we expected. Why?

Income	Annual Budget	Actual YTD Jan–Aug	% Budgeted Amount Target 67%	Projected to year end	% of Budgeted Amount Target 100%
Net Income	$240	($28,427)		($30,828)	

As you see from the next budget excerpt, this cash flow problem is created, in part, by a $70,000 grant balance due from the state, so a portion of this deficit was expected at this time of year.

Income	Annual Budget	Actual YTD Jan–Aug	% Budgeted Amount Target 67%	Projected to year end	% of Budgeted Amount Target 100%	Notes
State grants/ contracts	$171,000	$85,000	50%	$155,000	91%	$70K grant due 9/30

Unfortunately, the organization is also lagging behind on other income and exceeding projected expenses, including a big jump in health insurance premiums, more volunteers asking for mileage reimbursements, and an unplanned increase in professional services costs.

Expenses	Annual Budget	Actual YTD Jan–Aug	% Budgeted Amount Target 67%	Projected to year end	% of Budgeted Amount Target 100%	Notes
Salary/benefits	$247,100	$164,000	66%	$258,325	105%	Health insurance increase; unfilled position in 4th quarter
Staff/volunteers	18,800	15,750	84%	20,500	109%	Weak economy; more volunteers claiming miles
Professional services	25,000	33,357	133%	36,000	144%	Includes legal fees; insurance will reimburse $10K next year

2. *What are we going to do about this deficit?* Several answers appear in the budget, as you'll see below. One open staff position will remain unfilled through December. Professional development costs have been cut. Contributions to the reserve fund will be suspended and the money used to pay bills.

Expenses	Annual Budget	Actual YTD Jan–Aug	% Budgeted Amount Target 67%	Projected to year end	% of Budgeted Amount Target 100%	Notes
Salary/benefits	$247,100	$164,000	66%	$258,325	105%	Health insurance increase; unfilled position in 4th quarter
Professional development	5,000	1,625	33%	3,200	64%	
Reserve fund	20,000	11,500	58%	11,500	58%	Due to shortfall putting less into reserves

These expense reductions, plus more aggressive year-end fundraising, will still result in a projected budget deficit of $30,828 by the end of the year (see next page).

Income	Annual Budget	Actual YTD Jan–Aug	% Budgeted Amount Target 67%	Projected to year end	% of Budgeted Amount Target 100%	Notes
Foundations	$27,500	$26,500	96%	$34,500	125%	3 proposals under review
Membership	12,500	5,470	44%	15,250	122%	Assumes year-end appeal = last year
Major gifts	15,000	3,500	23%	20,000	133%	Major = $500+; need year-end push
Board gifts	3,500	1,550	44%	5,000	143%	Asking for more gifts to offset state cuts

Income	Annual Budget	Actual YTD Jan–Aug	% Budgeted Amount Target 67%	Projected to year end	% of Budgeted Amount Target 100%
Net Income	$240	($28,427)		($30,828)	

3. Should we be worried about this? A cautious board member will view this as a potential crisis and demand immediate action, asking, "How can we increase income and cut expenses at the same time?"

A more optimistic one might say, "Our insurance company owes us $10,000 and we've already put $11,500 into reserves this year, so we have $21,500 available now or next year to reduce the deficit if we choose to dip into our reserve fund. When you factor in this money from reserves and the insurance payment, we end up with an operating deficit of about $9,300, which we can recoup next year if we show more discipline."

Expenses	Annual Budget	Actual YTD Jan–Aug	% Budgeted Amount Target 67%	Projected to year end	% of Budgeted Amount Target 100%	Notes
Professional services	25,000	33,357	133%	36,000	144%	Includes legal fees; insurance will reimburse $10K next year
Reserve fund	20,000	11,500	58%	11,500	58%	Due to shortfall putting less into reserves

"Yes," continues the optimistic board member, "the board needs to work harder at fundraising, both now and in the future—but in general, we should stay the course."

Income	Annual Budget	Actual YTD Jan–Aug	% Budgeted Amount Target 67%	Projected to year end	% of Budgeted Amount Target 100%	Notes
Membership	12,500	5,470	44%	15,250	122%	Assumes year-end appeal = last year
Major gifts	15,000	3,500	23%	20,000	133%	Major equals $500-plus; need year-end push
Board gifts	3,500	1,550	44%	5,000	143%	Asking for more gifts to offset state cuts

Both the cautious and the optimistic board member have expressed defensible positions, and the push and pull between them is the heart of effective governance.

The three questions highlighted here provide a good start to the budget conversation. Others might include, "At what point do we need to make further cuts?" and "Are we willing to dig deeper into reserves to cover the deficit?"

As for questions you shouldn't ask, consider the following: "Why aren't we shopping at ______? We could save a few dollars on office supplies" or "Why don't we use bulk mail for the year-end appeal? That would save a hundred dollars." Those details are best left to staff. As ever, your job is to remain high enough above the details to see the entire landscape.

CHAPTER 18

Capital vs. Operating Expenses

Big-Ticket Purchases

From time to time, nonprofits purchase items that will last for years and cost more than routine expenses: a vehicle, a piece of equipment, a parcel of land, a new building. These *capital purchases* or *capital expenditures* require a little more sophistication.

Because you're buying assets, these items show up on your balance sheet, which tracks what you own and what you owe, and also on your *capital* or *equipment budget*. However, capital costs don't usually appear on the operating budget, the financial document trustees tend to track most closely. The risk is that you may end up spending money—cost overruns, anybody?—you don't actually have, because the board isn't paying sufficient attention.

So as a first step, boards need to *authorize* these expenses. Many organizations place expenditure limits on staff, requiring trustee approval for contracts and payments above a certain amount, which varies widely depending on the size of the organization. By definition, many capital costs are large enough to require board engagement.

The conversation proceeds through a straightforward string of questions: Why do we need this item? Why do we need it now? How long can we expect it to last? Can we afford to maintain it? Do we need to own it? Is there a lease or rental option that would better meet our needs?

If you don't ask these questions, and ask them early enough, you can get into trouble, as evidenced by the following real-life example. At the urging of their new executive director, a nonprofit art center contracted with a private developer to build gallery space in a trendy neighborhood with lots of foot traffic. Visitor numbers shot up, as expected, but sales didn't follow. After months of financial losses and equivocation, the board eventually fired the executive director. Then, in the hopes of salvaging their own organization, they began merger negotiations with another nonprofit.

What went wrong? The decision to buy the property was based on financial projections that overestimated income—including art sales, space rental, and donations, all of which would have required additional staff—and underestimated costs. Rather than question these projections and the assumptions they were based on, the board was swept up in the excitement of the venture and trusted the assurances of staff. They led with their hearts, rather than their heads.

Then, when the financial reports showed the pattern getting worse—higher than projected expenses and lower than expected revenues—they didn't respond quickly enough to turn the ship around. Their lack of prudence helped create the crisis, but in the end the executive director paid a bigger price.

The next thing to consider with capital projects is *competitive bids*. What's your policy for initiating a *request for proposal* or *RFP* process? Will you ask for competitive proposals, or would you prefer to work with someone you know? In developing this policy, board questions might include:

- Are we required by any of our funding sources, such as government agencies, to put out an RFP and seek competitive bids?
- Would we prefer to work with a vendor we know and trust, even if the price is higher?
- Are there other considerations? For example, is it important for us to support local businesses? If we're building a facility, are we willing to pay more up front for a building that will use less energy—and save us money—in the future?

Finally, there's the question of budgeting and financing for capital expense. Let's say your local food bank needs a refrigerated truck to deliver produce. Through a trucking company, staff finds a used "reefer" for $50,000. An independent mechanic checks under the hood and pronounces it roadworthy and a fair deal. Your executive director comes to the board for authorization to make the purchase.

In addition to the questions listed above, a few more to ask when considering the purchase of this truck would be:

- How much money do we have in the capital budget?

Organizations with regular capital expenses, such as hospitals, transportation providers, and universities, often track capital costs separately so that their capital funds aren't spent on regular program costs such as salaries or marketing. These capital accounts can grow three ways: from interest earned on investment; from securing grants specifically for buildings, equipment, and other capital items; and by making regular transfers from the operating budget as money is available, much as you would build a general reserve fund. Indeed, this account is sometimes called a capital reserve.

- Do we have the self-discipline to allocate the cost over time and rebuild the reserve?

We're entering the world of depreciation, which can be a confusing place. Because big-ticket items are expected to last for several years, their cost is allocated as an expense over several years based on the IRS estimate of their useful life. Here's a simple example:

Let's say the food bank staff believes the $50,000 truck will last five years—this is the IRS standard for vehicles—so it would depreciate at the rate of $10,000 per year. That $10,000 expense shows up each year on the profit and loss statement, even though all the money was spent in the first year. In principle, it's a real expense. A disciplined organization takes $10,000 annually from other income sources and rebuilds the *capital reserve* fund, in effect paying itself back. At the end of five years they have enough money to retire the truck and buy a newer model.

- Do we have the cash to pay for this ourselves, or do we need to finance it with somebody else's money?

In this case, “somebody else’s money” could be a gift or a grant or a loan. Although paying for something outright is often the simplest approach, there are times when borrowing is both prudent and necessary, as we discuss in Chapter 21.

CHAPTER 19

How and Why to Read an Audit

If you ever purchased a used car, perhaps you asked a mechanic to look it over first. The mechanic lifted the hood, drove the car around the block, and checked the fluid levels. Then she talked you through her concerns and recommendations, pointing out things you needed to know.

A financial audit is a bit like having a mechanic, in this case a *certified public accountant (CPA)*, assess your financial statements. Auditors try out your safety systems. They search for leaks. And based on what they learn, they often prepare a *management letter* suggesting changes and improvements. An audit isn't merely an assessment of the accuracy of the numbers but rather an opportunity to identify and assess any irregularities that appear in your financial statements.

Notes accountant Fred Duplessis of Sullivan, Powers & Company, "We try to make sure the numbers on your financial statement match what you tell us happened during the time period covered by the audit. Because an audit is designed to identify and evaluate risks, we may test your financial systems—but if we can corroborate the numbers independently, we may not need to test those systems."

An accountant can assess your financial statements at several levels. A *compilation* is cursory: "We agree that this is a car," say Duplessis, using the automotive metaphor, "and that's about it." A *review* compares your organization to industry standards.

An *audit* goes even deeper. If you spend more than $500,000 in federal funding in a single year, you must conduct a *federal single audit*, which follows a mandated formula. A *financial statement audit* may be required by other government grantmakers, depending on the amount of money you receive. Your staff and finance committee should know the relevant thresholds. Other funders, such as charitable foundations, may require audits as well.

But whether an annual audit is required or not, once your organization reaches a certain size and complexity—maybe it's an annual budget of half a million dollars, or perhaps a lower budget with a complicated mix of grants and other income streams—a yearly audit is a smart idea. Smaller nonprofits should consider an audit every few years, especially if they've had significant turnover or changes in the lifestyle of longtime employees. These could be indicators of possible embezzlement.

Sometimes even the prospect of an audit can uncover mischief. Several years ago, an employee of Pioneer Courthouse Square, a nonprofit that manages a public park in Portland, Oregon, came forward just before the audit process began and admitted to embezzling almost $100,000. He knew the audit would show discrepancies, and those discrepancies would lead to him. The organization used this embarrassing incident as an opportunity to tighten up its financial systems.

When reviewing an audit, several items require your attention.

1) Audits begin with an *opinion letter.* Your goal is to receive an *unqualified opinion*—in other words, the auditor has no significant concerns or reservations regarding the financial statements. This one- to two-page letter contains very specific, standard language. Pay attention to the following parts:

- The first paragraph, which outlines the dates and financial statements audited.
- The third paragraph, which is most important and says something like, "In the opinion of the auditor, the statements represent fairly, in all material respects, the financial position of the organization in accordance with generally accepted accounting principles." In accountant-speak, this is the seal of approval: the data included in the audit are properly presented and appear to be accurate.

Here's a template for an opinion letter supplied by a local accounting firm:

We have audited the accompanying statement of financial position of the (CLIENT) as of (DATE) and the related statements of activities, functional expenses and cash flows of the year then ended. These financial statements are the responsibility of the (CLIENT)'s management. Our responsibility is to express an opinion on these financial statements based on our audit.

We conducted our audit in accordance with auditing standards generally accepted in the United States of America. Those standards require that we plan and perform the audit to obtain reasonable assurance about whether the financial statements are free of material misstatement. An audit includes examining, on a test basis, evidence supporting the amounts and disclosures in the financial statements. An audit also includes assessing the accounting principles used and significant estimates made by management, as well as evaluating the overall financial statement presentation. We believe that our audits provide a reasonable basis for our opinion.

In our opinion, the financial statements referred to above present fairly, in all material respects, the financial position of the (CLIENT) as of (DATE) and the changes in its net assets and its cash flows for the year then ended in conformity with accounting principles generally accepted in the United States of America.

2) If your organization has an audit, the next thing to review is the statement of *financial position* and *statement of activities.*

- If your financial statement compares the current year to the previous one, do you see any significant discrepancies between the two years? For example, you might notice a substantial change in your government funding or a big increase in health insurance costs. Has your financial manager highlighted these types of discrepancies? This is a great opportunity to ask questions.
- Based on the numbers, how would you rate your overall financial health? What's the value of your net assets? Have they grown over

the last year—in other words, has your organization operated at a profit?

3) Review the *functional expenses* and *cash flows*. Does anything jump out at you? Do you notice any anomalies? For example, are your fundraising expenses, as a percentage of your total budget, within a reasonable range? In the desire to appear efficient, says Duplessis, many organizations under-report their fundraising costs, which has become a "red flag" for the IRS.

4) All audits include *notes*. Pay attention to the *summary of significant accounting policies* and also any notes on cash, investments, receivables, leases, and other transactions. These notes may reveal more about the organization's financial management policies and procedures than anything else in the audit. Make sure you understand what they say.

Is there anything significant that happened during the past year—a new facility, the launch of a big new program—that is not reflected in the notes? Are there any potential conflicts of interest—maybe the executive director is married to your insurance broker—that need to be raised and included?

5) Is the document accompanied by a *management letter*, which summarizes the auditor's concerns and recommendations? Were there any *significant deficiencies* (less severe) or *material weaknesses* (more severe) that need to be addressed? How does the organization plan to deal with these findings? On the next page are the relevant paragraphs from a sample management letter:

A deficiency in internal control exists when the design or operation of a control does not allow management or employees, in the normal course of performing their assigned functions, to prevent, or detect and correct misstatements on a timely basis. A material weakness is a deficiency, or combination of deficiencies in internal control, such that there is a reasonable possibility that a material misstatement of the (CLIENT)'s financial statements will not be prevented, or detected and corrected on a timely basis. We consider the deficiencies so indicated in the accompanying Schedule of Deficiencies in Internal Control and Other Recommendations to be material weaknesses in internal control.

A significant deficiency is a deficiency, or a combination of deficiencies in internal control that is less severe than a material weakness, yet important enough to merit attention by those charged with governance. We consider the deficiencies so indicated in the accompanying Schedule of Deficiencies in Internal Control and Other Recommendations to be significant deficiencies.

In addition, we have noted other matters during our audit as indicated in the accompanying Schedule of Deficiencies in Internal Control and Other Recommendations that are opportunities for strengthening internal control and operating efficiency. We have discussed the recommendations with the staff during the course of fieldwork and some of the recommendations may have already been implemented.

When it comes to audits, Duplessis warns of what he calls "an expectations gap. It's not our job to set up good systems—that's management's job. Our work is to evaluate the financial statements. If the audit helps management create better financial systems, so much the better."

Let's face it: unless they turn up illegal behavior or gross incompetence, audits can be boring. Oil changes are boring, too—but if you don't change the oil, sooner or later your engine will seize up.

CHAPTER 20

Surprise, It's Not Just About Money

Your IRS Return

In recent years, the IRS rolled out the new, improved Form 990—the first major changes to the nonprofit return in a generation. One stated goal is to reduce the paperwork burden, but reality looks a little different: the 12-page form is followed by up to 16 supplemental schedules, depending on the size and financial complexity of your organization.

As a trustee, these changes affect your work in several ways:

Unlike your personal tax return, the nonprofit return is about a lot more than income and deductions. It also asks a range of questions about governance, performance, and evaluation, including:

- Do you document all board and committee meetings? How?
- How many voting members of the board are independent and free of conflicts of interest?
- Do you have a written conflict of interest policy? (If not, see Chapter 13.)
- Do you have a written whistle-blower policy for staff who report misbehavior?
- Do you have a policy for retention and destruction of documents: what you save, how long you save it, and when you shred it?
- How do you evaluate the impact of your programs? What data do you use to measure success?

If you're required to report on your governance and evaluation practices, the theory goes, maybe you'll make an effort to improve those practices.

Unlike your personal tax return, your nonprofit return is public information and readily available to anyone who wants to see it. This has been true for a long time—it's mandated by the IRS, and made easier in recent years thanks to GuideStar, which features more than 3.2 million digitized 990 forms (www.guidestar.org). The new Form 990 increases the emphasis on disclosure and transparency. Which additional documents, it asks, are available to the public? How about your financial statements? Your conflict of interest policy? Other governing documents? Your IRS return is yet another reminder that your organization is accountable to the community at large, not just your trustees, staff, or constituents.

How much do you pay senior employees? How about your trustees? In the wake of various scandals, executive compensation is a big deal, even for nonprofits. Even if your organization overworks and underpays the staff (nothing to be proud of), be prepared to share salary and benefits information. If you provide compensation to board members, you'll need to include that information, too.

Do you use contracted fundraisers for mailings, phone banks, or events? If so, you're required to disclose the financial arrangements. As with compensation, recent scandals have made the regulators (and the public) wary about fundraisers-for-hire.

Tell us about your assets. If you have an endowment, donor-advised funds, facilities, land, artwork, or other substantive assets, you'll need to provide details about earnings, losses, expenditures, and administrative costs.

Have you actually read the return? The IRS wants to know about the process your organization used to review the completed forms, and whether the board received and discussed the return before it was filed.

With all this in mind, the last thing you want to do is ignore or casually sign off on the form. In addition to fulfilling your legal responsibilities, by reading the return you'll probably learn a few things about your organization that you didn't know.

CHAPTER 21

Reserve Funds, Endowments, And Lines of Credit

Money in the Bank

When it comes to saving money, many of us have good intentions but considerably less self-discipline. This scenario plays out in more or less predictable ways. We all know friends and colleagues who haven't saved enough for emergencies, college, retirement, or even that big vacation they've dreamed about. One financial challenge—a layoff, a car accident, a hospital visit—and their options may be limited to borrowing, bankruptcy, or moving in (again) with Mom.

More than a few organizations, like many individuals and families, struggle to pay their expenses each month, even in the best of times. With that reality in mind, we offer the following advice, with the understanding that the transition from debt to financial discipline can be exceedingly difficult for many organizations.

Reserve funds. Financially healthy nonprofits build a formal *operating reserve*. For most groups, a reasonable goal is to have enough money saved to cover basic costs—payroll, taxes, insurance, rent, and so on—for three to six months

A useful variation is the *opportunity fund*, which is used to pay for specific kinds of unbudgeted expenses. For example, many private land trusts use these funds to close conservation land deals when deadlines are tight and they can't wait for grants or don't have time to mount a six-month fundraising campaign. As with any reserve fund, the replenishment rule applies: spend the money when needed, then rebuild the fund while waiting for the next big opportunity.

There are essentially three ways to create a reserve:

- Set aside a fixed amount or a percentage of your budget each month, in the same way many individuals fund their vacations or retirement accounts. Create a line item in your expense budget for *reserve fund contributions*. (See the sample budget in Chapter 16.) When financial times are tight, you may choose to draw from the reserve, but do your best to develop the discipline to save when you can.
- Dedicate any unrestricted windfalls, such as unexpected gifts or bequests, to your reserve. If you exceed income projections for the year, consider putting some of the additional money in reserves.
- Organize a fundraising campaign to build your reserves. This effort requires a sophisticated pitch—many contributors want you to spend their money on immediate mission-related activities, rather than bank it—but your community includes sophisticated donors who understand the ways in which financially strong nonprofits are able to deliver the mission more efficiently and effectively.

For example, the Five Valleys Land Trust in Missoula, Montana, successfully completed a $500,000 campaign to build their "opportunity fund," which they use to protect land for conservation, recreation, and agriculture. Half of this total was provided by a challenge grant; the balance was raised by board and staff over the course of a year. Although the campaign had ups and downs like any other, donors were enthusiastic about the chance to help the organization increase its financial strength and program flexibility.

Endowments. An endowment is a reserve fund under lock and key, with an imposing lock and a fussy key. The *principal* or *corpus* is invested and, if invested well, generates income that can be reinvested or used for operational expenses. You can't *invade the principal* (i.e., spend any of it) except under highly specific (usually end-of-organizational-life) circumstances defined when the endowment is created.

Anyone who ever served on a nonprofit board has had endowment fantasies. "Why don't we have an endowment?" asks the trustee, as if it were something you could pick up at the store with a quart of milk. Three possible answers to this question include:

1) You're not ready. Endowment gifts rarely come from strangers. They are typically given by loyal donors who have been cultivated, have given for years, and have upgraded their gifts over time. If you don't have a functioning program to raise major gifts from individuals, it's tough to succeed with an endowment campaign. You need to walk before you can run; your group may still be learning to crawl.

2) Endowments are forever, and you're trying to work yourselves out of a job. Some nonprofits, such as universities, religious institutions, and hospitals, can make the case for having a forever mission. Others, like many disease-prevention organizations, are trying to cure the disease and put themselves out of business.

Imagine a domestic violence or homeless shelter launching an endowment campaign. Consider the message they're giving, intentional or not: We need an endowment—which is perpetual—because we never expect to solve this problem. Isn't that the wrong message?

3) Endowments can make you lazy. A well-established cultural organization in a major East Coast city receives more than 50 percent of its annual budget from endowment income. Pretty nice, right? The problem is, over the years, the institution became disconnected from its community and lost local support because they had no pressing need to reach out and ask. As the executive director told us, "We lost the ability to make clear to people that we actually need support." Fundraising is market research, and if you don't have to raise money, it's easy to lose touch with your constituents and their hopes, needs, and concerns.

Having said all that, endowments can provide a more-or-less predictable stream of income while positioning your organization as an institution with long-term vision and gravitas.

Lines of credit. A line of credit is a predetermined amount that a borrower can tap into as required, then repay as cash becomes available. Credit lines are often used by nonprofits to pay staff and expenses in advance of receiving a grant or payment for services already provided.

Many trustees and staff are understandably wary about borrowing money. There are moments, however, when it can be both prudent and necessary. Imagine that your primary government funding is a reimbursement contract: You get paid *after* the work is completed. In the course of completing the work, you run into cash-flow problems. Under these circumstances, would you rather default on the grant—and write off the work you've already done and the money you've already spent—or take out a loan?

If you have a reserve fund, you can borrow from your own organization. Lacking a reserve, you can approach a bank, credit union, community loan fund, or even an individual donor. Set up your line of credit *before* you need the money—when you're solvent and your cash flow is good—since it will be much easier to qualify for credit.

CHAPTER 22

Training the Board

Yes, This Is Everyone's Job

No one emerges from the womb as a fully formed board member, and even fewer are born with the innate ability to make sense of financial statements. Most of us find figures, flow charts, and spreadsheets to be incomprehensible, scary, or both. To recruit people for your board without defining the job first, and without offering ongoing tools and training, is a bit like transporting them to a deserted island with the parting words, "Find your way home."

Nearly all successful boards have some sort of job description or board agreement or board contract that identifies and explains expectations. The best of these documents are reciprocal: they define what is expected of you as a trustee and also what you can expect in return.

For example, by joining the board you've accepted fiduciary responsibility for your organization. Alas, if you don't understand the financial statements, you can't do your job. You have the inalienable right to insist on appropriate education and support—and this expectation needs to be spelled out in the agreement:

Board member responsibilities	**What board members can expect in return**
I accept fiduciary responsibility for the organization and will oversee its financial health and integrity.	I expect timely, accurate, and complete financial statements to be distributed at least quarterly, one week in advance of the relevant board meeting. I also expect to be trained to read and interpret these financial statements.

What's the proper level of training and support? Each organization must answer this question based on its culture, available resources, and the needs of the trustees, but here are a few ideas to get you started.

Board orientation book. Many organizations give incoming board members a three-ring binder with copies of the bylaws, articles of incorporation, board agreement, list of committees and their functions, minutes from recent meetings, an annual report, and the like. Nearly every organization includes financial data, but they seldom provide instructions on how to use the data to be an effective trustee. If you have a board orientation packet, include how-to materials that cover financial management skills for board members. (A copy of this book might be a good place to start.)

Regular board trainings. At least once a year, reserve a block of time at a board meeting or retreat. Ask your treasurer or finance manager or accountant to walk everyone through the financial statements, line by line, discussing the implications and answering questions. This process could easily take sixty to ninety minutes, so plan accordingly. In choosing your presenter, don't focus on title or credentials but on how well she can engage the participants and effectively translate the numbers for novices.

Peer mentoring. Pair up skilled trustees with those who have less experience or are less comfortable with financial analysis. The mentor's tasks would include an informal, one-on-one training session, debriefing phone calls after board meetings, and being available to answer questions as needed.

"What if" agenda items. This is sometimes called scenario planning. What if we lose our big grant? What if a board member offers to loan us money? What if our facility is shut down due to a flood? What if somebody dies and leaves us a big bequest? What if our executive director ends up in the hospital for six months?

Each of these conversations is a board training opportunity, a teachable moment before you have to make a real decision. You don't want to encourage trustee paranoia or stoke people's fantasies, but rather develop contingency plans before you need to use them.

CHAPTER 23

Developing the Next Generation of Nonprofit Financial Geniuses (Like You)

How long will it take before your organization can declare victory? If you're working to end hunger, how soon will everyone in your community have enough food? If you're fighting disease, when do you foresee a cure, or perhaps a prevention strategy everyone understands and uses? If you're promoting an end to racism and bigotry, when will you be able to claim success, shut down, and go home? In other words, do you really expect to be around for the victory party?

For many of us, our work will take decades to bear fruit. Who will carry on in your place? If you're not recruiting and training and supporting your replacement today, will she be available tomorrow?

We may be stretching the definition a little, but *fiduciary responsibility* is about ensuring the long-term health and viability of your organization. That responsibility doesn't end when you have money in the bank and an efficient accounting system. Without long-term leadership development, there's no long-term achievement. If you don't have a *succession plan* to engage and develop the next generation of financially literate trustees, you risk losing what you've worked so hard to create.

To develop a financial leadership succession plan, encourage others to learn by developing new skills. How about requiring a different board member to present the financial report at each board meeting? After everyone has taken a turn, we guarantee that you'll have a more financially literate board.

Consider term limits as a way of refreshing your board. Nonprofits are growing, changing organisms, and they need leaders who can envision the future in different ways. If your board composition doesn't change, organizational vision remains the same—and that can be deadly. Indeed, it's often the people with financial skills who stay too long, because they are perceived to be the hardest to replace. By developing financial literacy across the board, it's easier to create healthy turnover.

What's your vision for the organization, post-you? How do you define the financially healthy, successful nonprofit you hope to hand to the next generation? What benchmarks will you use to measure progress on renewing the organization and its leadership? This could be a great topic for a board retreat.

▶ ▶ ▶

Imagine we run into each other in the grocery store a few years from now. We're hanging out with the avocados and tomatoes, discussing the best way to make guacamole. I'm advocating for lots of garlic sautéed in butter. You like fresh-squeezed lemon juice.

"Are you still on that board?" I ask.

"Yes, but this is my last year."

"How's it going?"

"Really well. The financials are in order, we've got money in the bank, the programs are stronger, and we recruited some terrific new trustees."

"Wow, that's impressive. How do you feel about stepping down?"

"You know, I'll miss it," you say. "To be honest, there are parts I won't miss, but I'm leaving the organization in better shape than I found it. That feels good."

We both nod and smile. You reach for the garlic, I grab a few lemons, and as we're heading toward the check-out line I turn to you once again.

"I'm writing a book on financial management for board members. Can you offer any words of wisdom?"

You don't even hesitate, which is *really* impressive. "Tell people not to be scared. It's just math, and once you get past the math, it's mostly common sense."

"That's it?"

"Pretty much. And don't be afraid to ask a lot of questions. What's that quote? 'Half of being smart is knowing what you don't know.' Your readers should remember that."

"Thanks," I say. "That's helpful. And thanks for everything you do."

Appendix A • Income Planning Form

	Last year's actuals		Current year budget		Goal for 20__	
	Income ($)	% of total income	Income ($)	% or total income	Income ($)	% of total income
Foundations						
Corporations						
Government						
Member dues and donations						
Board giving						
Major donors (as you define)						
Benefit events						
Earned income (sales, fees, etc.)						
Investment and interest						
Other (specify)						
Totals	**$**	**100%**	**$**	**100%**	**$**	**100%**

Adapted from the Institute for Conservation Leadership, www.icl.org. Used with permission.

Appendix B • Managing Money: Who Does What?

Financially speaking, there are tasks for generalists (like you) and tasks for specialists. Before we identify the "who" and start handing out job titles, let's consider the "what"—the breadth of financial management responsibilities in a healthy nonprofit.

The following summary of tasks is intended to spark a conversation within your organization. While certain nonprofits will find some of these items irrelevant and other organizations will add to the list, it's a good place to start the discussion.

Handling income. Open and close bank accounts; handle cash; collect checks and tally online payments (through PayPal and the like); prepare and make bank deposits; transfer money between accounts.

Paying expenditures. Authorize, prepare, and sign checks; use the organization's credit card; make online payments; oversee petty cash.

Payroll management. Collect timesheets and compute payroll; oversee allocations of time by program or grant source; ensure compliance with personnel policies regarding vacation time and sick leave; pay payroll taxes.

Financial records and reports. Enter and maintain information on the organization's financial management software; create and post adjustments; reconcile bank statements; send invoices; prepare reports for funders; prepare and analyze financial statements; present this information to the staff, relevant committees, and the full board.

Budgeting. Develop, approve, and monitor the annual budget; prepare cash flow projections; create program budgets for grant proposals.

Financial decision-making. Develop short- and long-term financial plans; create a fundraising plan; create and monitor an investment policy.

Personnel policies. Set salary structure and benefits package; authorize raises and/or bonuses.

Annual report. Prepare tax returns (IRS Form 990); prepare records for an external review or audit; receive, review, and approve the auditor's report.

If you have any experience with risk management, you'll intuitively understand why it's important to divide these responsibilities among several people. For example, you probably don't want the same person authorizing, preparing, and signing checks above a certain amount, since this an invitation for everything from petty theft to grand larceny. Nor do you want only one person handling all your cash and deposits.

With that in mind, here's a generic take on job titles and job descriptions. Please note that there is no "one proper way" to do this—it's up to each organization to adapt these recommendations to their own needs, hopes, and limitations.

The treasurer. As a member of the board and chair of the finance committee, the treasurer is the volunteer overseer of all things financial. She works closely with the executive director and other staff on financial planning and budgeting, ensuring financial controls, and making sure the board has useful, accurate, and timely information. Other trustees often rely on the treasurer to help them make sense of the financial statements and guide them through the relevant discussions and decisions.

In most U.S. states, registered nonprofits are required to have either a treasurer or a chief financial officer (see below) with primary oversight over financial issues. In the case of large institutions with CFOs, there is some debate as to whether a treasurer is still necessary. In *Boards That Make a Difference*, governance guru John Carver calls the treasurer "a vestigial organ" that has lost its function in these larger, more sophisticated nonprofits. However, for most organizations, the role and responsibilities of the treasurer remain essential.

The bookkeeper. Somebody needs to add up the checks and other payments, prepare bank deposits, pay the bills, reconcile bank accounts, handle payroll accounting, and prepare draft financial statements. Once upon a time, this was all done in a series of journals or ledger books; hence the title "bookkeeper." Today, nearly everyone uses electronic spreadsheets or financial management programs such as QuickBooks or Peachtree, so the physical books are pretty much a thing of the past. What remains is the title, plus lots of data entry.

Bookkeeping functions are met several ways, depending on the size of the organization:

- All-volunteer organizations tend to rely on the treasurer to serve as bookkeeper.
- In nonprofits with only one employee, this work often falls to the executive director.
- Larger organizations may have a bookkeeper or the equivalent on staff.
- Many groups of all sizes use outside, independent bookkeepers to supplement staff and volunteers, and may also contract with external payroll service providers.

The executive director or CEO. Like it or not, financial management is a big part of the executive director's job. This includes sharing oversight responsibility with the board, hiring and supervising staff, financial and fundraising planning, developing and using budgets, managing cash flow, and understanding the accounting system well enough to use it for program evaluation. In smaller organizations with limited staff, it's especially important for the executive director to have a breadth of financial skills.

The business manager or finance director. You're most likely to find business managers in larger organizations or ones that rely on earned income, such as fees and ticket sales, and consequently operate more like businesses: affordable housing developers, performing arts organizations, nonprofit consulting and training organizations, community loan funds, museums, and so on.

It might help to think of this person as the chief accounting officer—someone with enough accounting wisdom to supervise the bookkeeper, make adjustments in the financial software records, prepare or correct financial statements, prepare the annual financial report, and work with an outside accountant to complete the tax return.

The chief financial officer. Nonprofit CFOs tend to work at larger institutions, such as hospitals and universities, which require complex financial, payroll, technology, and risk management systems. While the CFO supervises other financial staff, her primary role is as strategist and overseer, advising the CEO and board on long-term strategies for investment, growth, and making internal systems work more effectively.

The auditor. Auditors are *certified public accountants (CPAs)* who review your financial management systems to ensure you are complying with *generally accepted accounting principles*, or *GAAP.* Auditing firms provide different levels of analysis and service depending on your needs and budget. In most cases they include written recommendations for improvement.

The trustee. And where does this leave you: the all-purpose, generalist, utility-infielder board member? What's expected of you?

If you've read this far, you know the answer: Pay attention. Watch for discrepancies, irregularities, and things that don't make sense. Ask questions. Demand the training and support you need to fulfill your fiduciary responsibilities. And take financial management seriously.

Appendix C • Financial Functions Worksheet

TASK	RELATED TO	BK	FM	ED	T/FC	BD	0
Open mail/collect checks	Receipts						
Endorse checks	Receipts						
Prepare bank deposits	Receipts						
Make deposits	Receipts						
Open bank accounts	Receipts						
Transfer cash	Receipts						
Manage petty cash	Disbursements						
Receive/review invoices	Disbursements						
Approve vendor payments	Disbursements						
Store blank checks	Disbursements						
Prepare checks	Disbursements						
Approve staff reimbursements	Disbursements						
Purchase big-ticket items	Disbursements						
Sign a lease or contract	Disbursements						
Sign checks	Disbursements						
Authorize payroll	Personnel						
Compute payroll	Personnel						
Authorize vacation/sick time	Personnel						
Pay payroll taxes	Personnel						
Authorize staff salaries	Personnel						
Decide on benefits	Personnel						
Reconcile bank accounts	Records/Reports						
Prepare financial statements	Records/Reports						
Proof financial statements	Records/Reports						
Approve financial statements	Records/Reports						

Table: BK = Bookkeeper, FM = Finance Manager, ED = Executive Director, T/FC = Treasurer or Finance Committee, Bd = Board, O = Other

Appendix C • Financial Functions Worksheet *(Continued)*

TASK	RELATED TO	BK	FM	ED	T/FC	BD	0
Arrange for audit	Records/Reports						
Prepare IRS Form 990	Records/Reports						
Review IRS From 990	Records/Reports						
Prepare cash flow projections	Records/Reports						
Review cash flow projections	Cash management						
Excess cash investment decisions decisions	Cash management						
If cash tight, payment priorities	Cash management						
Apply for a loan	Cash management						
Approve a loan	Cash management						
Prepare grant proposal budgets	Grant management						
Prepare bills to funding sources	Grant management						
Prepare reports to founders	Grant management						
Prepare annual budget	Grant management						
Approve annual budget	Grant management						
Monitor budgets amounts	Grant management						

Table: BK = Bookkeeper, FM = Finance Manager, ED = Executive Director, T/FC = Treasurer or Finance Committee, Bd = Board, 0 = Other

Appendix D • Mapping an Alternative Route

Using Contingency Budgets

Unless you're involved with a brand new nonprofit, your financial journey crosses landscapes you've probably seen before. Health care costs keep rising, foundations delay their grant decisions, the economy cycles, the legislature looks for programs to cut, you can't seem to find good development staff, and most large donations don't arrive until the end of the year, which messes up your cash flow.

The story of a statewide New England nonprofit offers a cautionary tale. When three major funders refused to renew their grants in the same year, the organization folded. In retrospect, says a former trustee, "The board approved a budget that was more fragile than we realized. We didn't create a worst-case scenario. We didn't 'stress test' the business model." In other words, the organization hadn't prepared a contingency budget.

Contingency budgets describe different income and expense scenarios side by side, allowing you to develop a Plan B before you need it. On the next page is an example for Neighbors Helping Neighbors, starting with income.

Despite government cuts of about 20%, this contingency budget is designed to reduce overall income by only 10%. To replace a portion of the lost government revenue, this scenario emphasizes other fundraising strategies such as major gifts, membership development, and foundation grants. In good times, this is a path worth exploring because it yields a broader mix of income. In hard times, when dependency on government funding can be a liability, it's essential. On page 108, let's see how this model works with expenses.

Appendix D • Mapping an Alternative Route *(Continued)*

Using Contingency Budgets

Income	Approved budget	Scenario: Government funds cut 20%	Contingency budget	Notes
State grants and contracts	$171,000	($36,000)	$135,000	Current estimate from legislative committee
City/county grants	95,000	(15,000)	80,000	Applying for full amount, officials not encouraging
Foundations	27,500	7,000	34,500	Greater outreach, more proposals
Membership	12,500	3,750	16,250	Greater outreach to donors
Major gifts	15,000	5,000	20,000	See previous note
Board Gifts	3,500	1,500	5,000	See previous note
Benefit events	18,000	(2,500)	15,500	Small venue this year, less revenue potential
Investment	3,240		3,240	
TOTAL	**$345,740**	**($36,250)**	**$309,490**	

Appendix D • Mapping an Alternative Route *(Continued)*

Expenses	Approved budget	Scenario: Government funds cut 20%	Contingency budget	Notes
Salary and benefits	$247,100		$247,100	No pay cuts for staff
Occupancy (rent/ utilities)	15,600		15,600	
Telephone and Internet	1,600		1,600	
Postage/shipping	2,000	400	2,400	Larger year-end mailing equals higher postage but greater net income
Printing	3,000	350	3,350	See previous note; goal to diversify income and reduce grant reliance
Office supplies	1,200	(50)	1,150	
Mileage and travel	18,800	(6,300)	12,500	If necessary, reduce reimbursement for volunteers
Insurance	5,200		5,200	
Professional development	5,000	(2,500)	2,500	Staff poll: cut professional development before salaries
Professional services	25,000	(8,500)	16,500	Reduce bookkeeper hours, cut contract event coordinator, clean office ourselves
Miscellaneous	1,000	(200)	800	
TOTAL	**325,500**	**(16,800)**	**308,700**	
Reserve	20,000	(14,000)	6,000	Reserve fund target is 5% of annual budget; reduced but not eliminated
Total plus reserve	**345,500**	**(30,800)**	**314,700**	
NET CASH	**$240**	**($5,450)**	**($5,210)**	

As with the income side, the budget planners didn't merely add or subtract 10% from each line item to reach their goal. Rather, they looked at the breadth of operations and made judgments about where funds could reasonably be cut and where additional money might be usefully spent. Given the already low salaries paid by grassroots nonprofits such as Neighbors Helping Neighbors, they chose to reduce other expenses and raise new revenues before cutting staff pay and benefits.

Budget reductions of 10% may not be large enough to trigger wholesale changes, so this example doesn't include eliminating programs, mergers, or anything that dramatic. However, this template works for deeper budget reductions, if needed. You can also create contingency budgets to help prepare for unanticipated bequests, grants, or other unexpected income.

Before the money appears or disappears, ask yourselves:

- How would our budget change under different scenarios—and what are those scenarios likely to be? For example, if we have to cancel our big benefit due to the weather, how would we respond? What if we receive an unexpected bequest? How about if our development director leaves and we can't fill the position for six months?
- What events would trigger a shift from one contingency to another—the loss of a major grant? A big increase in health insurance? A lawsuit?
- When reviewing our monthly or quarterly projections, how far off do we need to be to begin implementing Plan B?

This sort of budget planning is best completed in the calm before the storm. Once the crisis hits (or in better times, when the money magically appears), you'll have a harder time making rational decisions. Contingency budgets work best if you create them before you really need them.

Appendix E • Board Financial Management Quiz

Take the quiz before you read this book. Can you answer these questions without referring to your board materials?

1. What is your organization's annual budget?
2. What are your current sources of income—and what would be the best mix of income for your organization? (Take a look at Appendix A, the income planning form)
3. What are your largest expenses? What percentage of the budget do they consume?
4. Does your organization have a reserve fund? How much money is in it, and under what circumstances can it be used?
5. What is your biggest financial risk?
6. How do you use financial management tools to measure your impact? Does your organization compute the cost per unit of service: for example, for each client you help, or audience member you entertain, or acre you protect?
7. What would help you to better understand your organization's financial situation?

Gratitude

Many thanks to our colleagues who shared their wisdom on all things financial: Jean Block, JoAnne Caswell, Fred Duplessis, Steve Gold, Anne Gould, Ben Gregory, Linda LaFrance, Judy Levine, Miriam Levitt, Linda Markin, Peggy Mathews, Jan Masaoka, Terry Miller, Larry Murphy, Dan Petegorsky, Jayne Sheridan, Kay Sohl, and Barbara Wagner. We are grateful for their expertise, professionalism, and good humor.

Thanks also to Katherine Arnup and Jan Waterman for their love and support during the creation of this book.

About the Authors

Andy Robinson (www.andyrobinsononline.com) provides training and consulting for nonprofits in fundraising, grantseeking, board development, marketing, earned income, planning, leadership development, and facilitation. Over the past 16 years, Andy has worked with organizations in 47 US states and Canada. He specializes in the needs of groups working for human rights, social justice, environmental conservation, arts, and community development. Andy is the author of several books including *How to Raise $500 to $5,000 from Almost Anyone* and *Great Boards for Small Groups*, both available from Emerson & Church, Publishers (www.emersonandchurchcom). *Grassroots Grants* and *Selling Social Change* are published by Jossey-Bass. When he's not on the road, he lives in Plainfield, Vermont.

Nancy Wasserman is the Principal of Sleeping Lion Associates (www.sleepinglion.net), a consulting firm that works with mission-driven ventures to identify, analyze and address key strategic questions and then develop plans for implementing new programs or ventures. She has helped dozens of businesses, nonprofits, cooperatives and government agencies better understand their financials, prepare feasibility analyses and develop business and program plans. Nancy has extensive experience with groups working in social finance, sustainable development, energy efficiency, agriculture, and affordable housing. She divides her time between Montpelier, Vermont, and Ottawa, Ontario.

Copies of this and other books from the publisher are available at discount when purchased in quantity for boards of directors or staff. Call 508-359-0019 or visit www.emersonandchurch.com

15 Brook Street • Medfield, MA 02052
Tel. 508-359-0019 • Fax 508-359-2703
www.emersonandchurch.com